God Has No Grandchildren

God Has No Grandchildren

A Guided Reading of
Pope Pius XI's Encyclical
Casti Connubii
(On Chaste Marriage)

LEILA MARIE LAWLER

AROUCA
PRESS

ISBN: 978-1-989905-60-9 (pbk)
ISBN: 978-1-989905-61-6 (hardcover)

Arouca Press
PO Box 55003
Bridgeport PO
Waterloo, ON N2J3G0
Canada
www.aroucapress.com
Send inquiries to info@aroucapress.com

Cover design by John Folley
Cover: *Marriage at Cana*
by Giotto (John 2:1–11)

"So God created man in his own image, in the image of God created he him; male and female created he them.... Therefore shall a man leave his father and his mother, and shall cleave unto his wife: and they shall be one flesh."

Genesis 1:27; 2:24

"Have you not read that from the beginning the Creator 'made them male and female' and said, 'For this reason a man shall leave his father and mother and be joined to his wife, and the two shall become one flesh'? So they are no longer two, but one flesh. Therefore, what God has joined together, no human being must separate."

Matthew 19:4–6

"This is a great mystery: but I speak concerning Christ and the church."

Ephesians 5:32

TABLE OF CONTENTS

ACKNOWLEDGMENTS

If it weren't for my comrade-in-arms Susan Almeda, I would have taken even longer to get around to reading this remarkable encyclical. Catholics of our post-Vatican II era tend to focus on *Humanae Vitae* when we speak about marriage, a conversation which we narrow to the issue of contraception. Read in the light of *Casti Connubii*, the full and beautiful *context* of that document emerges.

I thank Mary Brennan for her sharp eye and encouragement, and my daughters Rosie Turner, Suzanne Saur, and Deirdre Folley for editorial and filial support. I am grateful to my son-in-law, John Folley, for the cover design.

I am grateful for Peter Kwasniewski's encouragement and indispensable help with publishing this expanded version as a real book you can hold in your hands.

FOREWORD

If the treasure contained in the field is our
Catholic faith, a jewel discovered there is certainly *Casti Connubii*. So many years after its
publication, it still speaks profoundly about
the gift of marriage and the family. Published at a very different time in 1930, and
with expressions perhaps a little difficult to
comprehend in our own times, it needs a guide
to help us grasp its content.

This small book provides that guide, that
key to understanding. May Mrs. Lawler's
book assist in shining the light on this often
overlooked encyclical, which explains so well
God's mystery of marriage and the family.

✠ George Cardinal Pell

PREFACE TO THE SECOND EDITION

I began this close reading of the encyclical *Casti Connubii* in an attempt to go to the root of what marriage is, as taught by the Catholic Church. In these pages you will find amplification and explanation of the text of that encyclical. The reader can follow along with the original text, provided here.

In the intervening time since publishing this book's first edition, consternation continues to grow regarding the teaching from Pope Francis, most notably in the Apostolic Exhortation *Amoris Laetitia;* confusion seems to reign, confusion that exists not only in the minds of the faithful but in the actual governance of the Church.

We see some dioceses upholding the teachings as previously understood and expressed in Canon Law (whether in practice as well as in law is another question); we see other dioceses and even whole Bishops' Conferences interpreting the document in ways not consistent with Scripture (specifically, Matthew 5:31–32 Matthew 19:4–9 and Luke 16:18, passages not cited in *Amoris Laetitia* at all).

At the end of the book, therefore, I have added a section that I hope brings out developments – and contradictions – of the perennial (but admittedly terse) teaching contained in Pope Pius XI's *Casti Connubii* in paragraph 10. This section will of necessity have a different tone from that of the rest of the book. Nevertheless, I hope the reader will peruse it in order to clarify his thoughts on ways in which new emphases and interpretations affect what is the most fundamental institution we have been given, the family.

As I read commentaries from various sources on *Amoris Laetitia*, I am frustrated by a dearth of references, even from its critics, to teachings preceding *Familiaris Consortio*. As important as that document is, it is only one document of moderate length, summarizing many principles of primary importance to marriage and the family. And as a quick glance at its footnotes will confirm, that exhortation itself indicates a reliance – as of course it must – on the teachings of previous documents and of Scripture.

We can only free ourselves from the dangerous assumption that new expressions of doctrine may overturn the previous Magisterium rather than amplify it (even if claiming to be development *only*) if those who seek to guard tradition consciously and intentionally retain the freedom (and duty) to reference teachings of the past. It seems more important than ever that commentators not take for granted, but make explicit, that the Magisterium of the Church ought to demonstrate that *any* articulation of doctrine must rely on and maintain continuity with the teachings that preceded it.

We desperately need an infusion of the old, strong tonic of the past, the more our leaders seem to embrace leaving it behind. As G. K. Chesterton says, "A thing as old as the Catholic Church has an accumulated armoury and treasury to choose from; it can pick and choose among the centuries and brings one age to the rescue of another. It can call in the old world to redress the balance of the new."

And after all, *Casti Connubii* is not so very old, as things are reckoned in the Church. In its time, the difficulties of today were already on the rise (as one can see by looking at the included timeline of events leading up to the encyclical). The bracing effect of Pius XI's blunt commentary may be the very remedy to the destabilization, equivocation, and confusion of our present day.

Leila M. Lawler
January 17, 2021

GOD HAS NO GRANDCHILDREN

INTRODUCTION

For the past seven hundred years or so, our civilization has been engaged in a project that might be called modernism, or self-actualization, or the re-inventing of human nature. Another name for it could be Loss of Memory.

At *Like Mother, Like Daughter*, the website that I write with my daughters, we have a phrase that sums up what we consider to be the proper response: "It's important to maintain the collective memory."

We began by just wanting to know what the others were doing, now that the daughters are grown and have moved away. A blog seemed like a good solution for sharing things visually so we'd be able to talk about our adventures.

But this "collective memory" soon took on another, more universal dimension and resonated with our readers. We began to speak of the wisdom that comes only from experience, wisdom that once lost, is hard to recover.

The Catholic Church is the longest lasting and best guardian of the collective memory there is. Her life has its origins in the beginning, at Creation, and reaches its fulfillment in Jesus Christ, Who, by the laying on of hands, one High Priest to another, step by step to our day, uniquely transmits her wisdom and grace, and the life of Christ, to her members.

Some years ago, on our website, I suggested reading a document of the Church called *Casti Connubii*, which means On Chaste Marriage (or Wedlock), written by Pope Pius XI in 1930. I called it a document that "might possibly be considered the most retrograde, dusty, and shockingly old-fashioned bit of unwanted advice ever to be foisted on a mocking world."

Why? Why would I undertake this sort of project on a blog devoted mainly to seemingly more mundane pursuits, like cooking, cleaning, and quilting? Because ... I saw a need to answer a few questions. What is marriage? What is my vocation? How will I know?

If marriage is a vocation, it leads to the next question, which is (thinking of the many needs of the world and of those around us): "Where can I do the most good?"

The question of *what marriage is* gets buried under all kinds of tugs-of-war amongst people who might be anxious or only thinking about what they might want. Here I don't even really have in mind the current issue of same-sex marriage. I'm more pondering the confusion and ignorance about goals – and consequent heartache – of people in general.

Is marriage an elevated kind of roommate situation, wherein the subjects save a lot of money on rent, but have to accept haggling over household chores as a necessary evil?

Is it a self-fulfillment quest? Something so individual it involves no one but the principals?

Is it a losing proposition, doomed by its premise (two people even being able to stand each other for an ever-lengthening life-span)?

You can see where the confusion sets in.

I especially want to help women (and thus the men who love us) answer the burning question of how *God* prioritizes the good that we wish to do, and how we would know.

After all, the resolution to the conflict we feel about how to use our talents and energy will remain subjective, and thus *un*resolved, until we can determine an objective answer; that is, God's will and plan.

There is another pressing question as I write, which arises now that the pope has determined to address the issue of marriage in another Synod. Some think that Pope Francis' approach is to treat society as essentially pagan, having very little knowledge of what constitutes a true union. The evidence for such

a position is strong, after all. The sexual revolution has created a situation in which pursuit
of self-fulfillment trumps all other consider-
ations. One could argue that even pagans of
ancient times had more understanding of how
marriage builds society. This view, apparently
that of Pope Francis, posits that perhaps the
majority of marriages, in Church and out, are
basically fraudulent and invalid.

Some criticize this view as offending against
the principle that good and upright living is
open to ordinary people, that one need not
be a saint with a degree in moral theology to
have a valid marriage, and that the sacrament
will overcome failures in human understanding. The Church has always held that marriage is to be presumed valid—even marriages
between unbaptized persons.[1] Certainly one
would not wish to argue that with God, something as important and utterly fundamental

---

1   There is a distinction between marriage as a natural state and as a sacrament, and understanding the
question can be tricky. Marriage between non-baptized
persons who have the basic intent to make a lifelong
commitment, open to children, is presumed valid, that
is, real, but not sacramental; this is also called "natural
marriage." The marriage of Catholics to each other, or
the marriage of Catholics to non-Catholic Christians,
is also presumed to be sacramental, perfecting natural marriage, when carried out according to canonical
form. The marriage of *baptized* non-Catholics is also
considered sacramental. Consult the *Catechism of the
Catholic Church* (or a good canon lawyer) for more
information.

to human life as forming a human family is nigh impossible – in our age or in any other.

However, I would argue that something important is left out of both these views, each of which has its merits. For human beings, even the most natural processes require a certain amount of education. Unlike the animals, we can't do things by instinct. Unlike the angels, we require mediating help from the cosmos, history, the culture, the saints, and the Church. It's a precept of theology that grace builds on nature and doesn't replace it.

We can neither be left to the hardness of our hearts as in Moses' time, offered an easy way out of difficulty that requires not much of our spirit but leaves us low on generosity; nor can we be left to muddle along as best we can, patted on the back with an insouciant "*gratia supplet*" (grace will supply your needs).

No. While we can believe in human nature and a human anthropology that writes good things in our hearts (St. Paul's letter to the Romans, 2:15), some must take the responsibility to *teach* – by word and by example – the others, giving them the helping hand and the proper formation that they simply must have when the forces of evil press around them.

After all, it should come as no surprise that today's assault on the peace of society is aimed directly at *this* institution – marriage, and its goods: children and the home. It won't do to leave people to their own devices, blindly hopeful that nature and grace will do their work. We can call on our priests and bishops, especially, to study and proclaim the truth about marriage in the crisis we face today. We can support those who do and pray for those who do not. We can speak out when necessary. All Christians must try to do our best in word and deed, to help each other.

* * *

So what is God's will for marriage? Is it possible to find out such a thing? I believe that it is.

The answers that the Church offers us are based on our nature and revelation, brought to us by this "collective memory" I speak of, both that of the faithful and that of the Church—the collective memory of which is what is called her Magisterium or teaching authority. Or, simply put, Scriptures and Sacred Tradition.

At the very least, even a non-Catholic or a person of uncertain faith will benefit from discovering what the Church really teaches, as opposed to what those outside the Church (perhaps for reasons of their own), say she does; or what the clumsiness of Catholic teachers, clergy and lay, obscure.

* * *

As an institution that helpfully publishes all her official teachings, the Catholic Church makes this discovery remarkably easy. There really ought to be no confusion about what she really thinks about practically anything. She has much to say about marriage and what a woman's role in "doing the most good" for society might be.

This encyclical (a word which simply means a longish letter referencing the continuous, united, and official teaching of the whole Church on a particular subject, as well as the Pontiff's particular application for the faithful at the time he is writing) precedes one you may have heard of, *Humanae Vitae*. That document expressed Church teaching on birth control and made some fairly specific and dire predictions, all of which, and more, have come to pass.

You might not be aware, even if you are Catholic, that every encyclical references those preceding it on its subject. No encyclical exists in a vacuum. The measure of a reliable and truly authoritative encyclical letter is its presentation of Catholic truth in solidarity with Tradition and Sacred Scripture — that "collective memory" I speak of.

Obviously, to read the encyclical you . . . just read it. What I am providing here, in addition to the text of the encyclical, is a reflection on each section that may give you some food for thought and discussion, as well as a little help over the difficult bits. For the most part, I am proceeding through the document in order, although there is a little jumping around.

And it may be that we have to suspend our tendency to doubt or to disbelieve, just long enough to read and comprehend.

Let's go slowly and talk about each section at a time. No rush.

Let's read *Casti Connubii* together with an open mind.

Want to give it a go?

EVENTS LEADING UP TO
CASTI CONNUBII

Human nature seems to require that each generation have the impression that social deterioration has just recently set in. Consulting a timeline of events leading up to the publication of this encyclical suggests otherwise. The following timeline is courtesy of the blog *Paths of Love* (https://www.pathsoflove.com/texts/casti-connubii-outline/).

1798	Thomas Malthus publishes *An Essay on the Principle of Population.*
1797–1830	Jeremy Bentham, James Mill, Francis, Robert Dale Owen propose contraception as a means for limiting population.
1853	Roman Penitentiary, asked about periodic abstinence to avoid children, allows it.
1855	Rubber condoms become available.

1816–1876   Roman Penitentiary and Holy Office repeatedly respond that contraceptive intercourse is wrong, and that passive cooperation in contraceptive intercourse is impermissible, unless there is danger of serious harm to the spouse (question was posed regarding the wife).

1857   Matrimonial Causes Act allows legal divorce in England in the case of adultery (or in the case of aggravated adultery when the wife seeks divorce).

1877   Charles Bradlaugh founds Malthusian League in England.

February 10, 1880   Pope Leo XIII publishes *Arcanum Divinae Sapientiae,* on Christian Marriage.

June 16, 1880   Roman Penitentiary proposes that confessors suggest period abstinence to couples practicing contraception.

1880–1920   Medical profession debates the desirability of contraceptives, with increasing approval.

1896   Connecticut prohibits marriage for the "epileptic, imbecile or feeble-minded." In following years other States make similar laws.

1907   Indiana allows sterilization
for eugenic reasons.
Other states follow.

1900–1930   Push in England for
enforced sterilization
for eugenic purposes.

1908   Lambeth Conference (Anglican)
rejects artificial contraception.

1910   Divorce legalized in Portugal.

1913   Margaret Sanger (USA) begins
publishing *The Woman Rebel*
(promoting contraception).

1914–1918   World War I, with its
displacement of countless
people, its horrors, and the
disillusionment of many
with European "values,"
not to mention the loose
morals that go with war.

1920   Lambeth Conference (Anglican)
rejects artificial contraception.

1921   Margaret Sanger founds the
American Birth Control League.

1923   Matrimonial Causes Act of
July 18 gives equal divorce
rights to men and women,
allowing divorce in any case of
adultery (without collusion).

1927   U.S.A. Supreme court
upholds state laws mandating
compulsory sterilization.

June, 1930 "Revolutionierung der Ehe," in the German Catholic periodical *Hochland* calls for reconsideration of Catholic teaching on contraception.

August 15, 1930 Lambeth Conference (Anglican) accepts contraception when there is great need (193 votes for, 67 against, 46 abstaining).

October 4, 1930 Cardinal Francis Bourne, Archbishop of Westminster, condemns the Lambeth decision.

October 30, 1930 King Boris III of Bulgaria (Orthodox) marries Princess Giovanna of Italy (Catholic).

December 24, 1930 Pope Pius XI announces the encyclical in the Christmas Eve Sermon to the Cardinals and Prelates of the Roman Curia.

December 31, 1930 Pope Pius XI issues the Encyclical *Casti Connubii*

THE TEXT
of the
ENCYCLICAL

CASTI CONNUBII[1]
On Christian Marriage

Encyclical Letter of Pope Pius XI
December 31, 1930

Venerable Brethren and Beloved Children, Health and Apostolic Benediction.

How great is the dignity of chaste wedlock, Venerable Brethren, may be judged best from this, that Christ Our Lord, Son of the Eternal Father, having assumed the nature of fallen man, not only, with His loving desire of compassing the redemption of our race, ordained it in an especial manner as the principle and foundation of domestic society and therefore of all human intercourse, but also raised it to the rank of a true and great sacrament of the New Law, restored it to the original purity of its divine institution, and accordingly entrusted all its discipline and care to His spouse the Church.

2. In order, however, that amongst men of every nation and every age the desired fruits

---

1 [An outline of the encyclical is given in Appendix 2.]

may be obtained from this renewal of matrimony, it is necessary, first of all, that men's minds be illuminated with the true doctrine of Christ regarding it; and secondly, that Christian spouses, the weakness of their wills strengthened by the internal grace of God, shape all their ways of thinking and of acting in conformity with that pure law of Christ so as to obtain true peace and happiness for themselves and for their families.

3. Yet not only do We, looking with paternal eye on the universal world from this Apostolic See as from a watchtower, but you, also, Venerable Brethren, see, and seeing deeply grieve with Us, that a great number of men, forgetful of that divine work of redemption, either entirely ignore or shamelessly deny the great sanctity of Christian wedlock, or relying on the false principles of a new and utterly perverse morality, too often trample it under foot. And since these most pernicious errors and depraved morals have begun to spread even amongst the faithful and are gradually gaining ground, in Our office as Christ's Vicar upon earth and Supreme Shepherd and Teacher We consider it Our duty to raise Our voice to keep the flock committed to Our care from poisoned pastures and, as far as in Us lies, to preserve it from harm.

4. We have decided therefore to speak to you, Venerable Brethren, and through you to the

whole Church of Christ and indeed to the whole human race, on the nature and dignity of Christian marriage, on the advantages and benefits which accrue from it to the family and to human society itself, on the errors contrary to this most important point of the Gospel teaching, on the vices opposed to conjugal union, and lastly on the principal remedies to be applied. In so doing We follow the footsteps of Our predecessor, Leo XIII, of happy memory, whose Encyclical *Arcanum*,[2] published fifty years ago, We hereby confirm and make Our own, and while We wish to expound more fully certain points called for by the circumstances of our times, nevertheless We declare that, far from being obsolete, it retains its full force at the present day.

I. THE NATURE AND GOODS OF MARRIAGE

5. And to begin with that same Encyclical, which is wholly concerned in vindicating the divine institution of matrimony, its sacramental dignity, and its perpetual stability, let it be repeated as an immutable and inviolable fundamental doctrine that matrimony was not instituted or restored by man but by God; not by man were the laws made to strengthen and confirm and elevate it but by God, the Author of nature, and by Christ Our Lord

---

2   Encycl. *Arcanum divinae sapientiae*, 10 Febr. 1880.

by Whom nature was redeemed, and hence these laws cannot be subject to any human decrees or to any contrary pact even of the spouses themselves. This is the doctrine of Holy Scripture;[3] this is the constant tradition of the Universal Church; this the solemn definition of the sacred Council of Trent, which declares and establishes from the words of Holy Scripture itself that God is the Author of the perpetual stability of the marriage bond, its unity and its firmness.[4]

6. Yet although matrimony is of its very nature of divine institution, the human will, too, enters into it and performs a most noble part. For each individual marriage, inasmuch as it is a conjugal union of a particular man and woman, arises only from the free consent of each of the spouses; and this free act of the will, by which each party hands over and accepts those rights proper to the state of marriage,[5] is so necessary to constitute true marriage that it cannot be supplied by any human power.[6] This freedom, however, regards only the question whether the contracting parties really wish to enter upon matrimony or to marry this particular person; but the nature of matrimony is entirely independent of the

---

3   *Gen.*, I, 27–28; II, 22–23; Matth., XIX, 3 sqq.; *Eph.*, V, 23 sqq .
4   Conc. Trid., Sess. XXIV.
5   *Cod. iur. can.* [1917], c. 1081 & 2.
6   *Cod. iur. can.,* c. 1081 & 2.

free will of man, so that if one has once contracted matrimony he is thereby subject to its divinely made laws and its essential properties. For the Angelic Doctor, writing on conjugal honor and on the offspring which is the fruit of marriage, says: "These things are so contained in matrimony by the marriage pact itself that, if anything to the contrary were expressed in the consent which makes the marriage, it would not be a true marriage."[7]

7. By matrimony, therefore, the souls of the contracting parties are joined and knit together more directly and more intimately than are their bodies, and that not by any passing affection of sense or spirit, but by a deliberate and firm act of the will; and from this union of souls by God's decree, a sacred and inviolable bond arises. Hence the nature of this contract, which is proper and peculiar to it alone, makes it entirely different both from the union of animals entered into by the blind instinct of nature alone in which neither reason nor free will plays a part, and also from the haphazard unions of men, which are far removed from all true and honorable unions of will and enjoy none of the rights of family life.

8. From this it is clear that legitimately constituted authority has the right and therefore

---

7 S. Thom. Aquin., *Summa theol.*, Supplem. XLIX, art.3.

the duty to restrict, to prevent, and to punish those base unions which are opposed to reason and to nature; but since it is a matter which flows from human nature itself, no less certain is the teaching of Our predecessor, Leo XIII of happy memory:[8] "In choosing a state of life there is no doubt but that it is in the power and discretion of each one to prefer one or the other: either to embrace the counsel of virginity given by Jesus Christ, or to bind himself in the bonds of matrimony. To take away from man the natural and primeval right of marriage, to circumscribe in any way the principal ends of marriage laid down in the beginning by God Himself in the words 'Increase and multiply,'[9] is beyond the power of any human law."

9. Therefore the sacred partnership of true marriage is constituted both by the will of God and the will of man. From God comes the very institution of marriage, the ends for which it was instituted, the laws that govern it, the blessings that flow from it; while man, through generous surrender of his own person made to another for the whole span of life, becomes, with the help and cooperation of God, the author of each particular marriage, with the duties and blessings annexed thereto from divine institution.

---

8   Encycl. *Rerum novarum*, 15 May 1891.
9   *Gen.*, I, 28.

The Goods (i.e., Blessings) of Marriage

10. Now when We come to explain, Venerable Brethren, what are the blessings that God has attached to true matrimony, and how great they are, there occur to Us the words of that illustrious Doctor of the Church whom We commemorated recently in Our Encyclical *Ad salutem* on the occasion of the fifteenth centenary of his death:[10] "These," says St. Augustine, "are all the blessings of matrimony on account of which matrimony itself is a blessing: offspring, conjugal faith, and the sacrament [*proles, fides, sacramentum*]."[11] And how under these three heads is contained a splendid summary of the whole doctrine of Christian marriage, the holy Doctor himself expressly declares when he said: "By conjugal faith it is provided that there should be no carnal intercourse outside the marriage bond with another man or woman; with regard to offspring, that children should be begotten of love, tenderly cared for and educated in a religious atmosphere; finally, in its sacramental aspect that the marriage bond should not be broken and that a husband or wife, if separated, should not be joined to another even for the sake of offspring. This we regard as the law of marriage by which the fruitfulness of nature is adorned and the evil of incontinence is restrained."[12]

---

10   Encycl. *Ad salutem,* 20 April 1930.
11   St. August., *De bono coniug.,* cap. 24, n. 32.
12   St. August., *De Gen. ad litt.,* lib. IX, cap. 7, n. 12.

The Blessing of Offspring

11. Thus amongst the blessings of marriage, the child holds the first place. And indeed the Creator of the human race Himself, Who in His goodness wishes to use men as His helpers in the propagation of life, taught this when, instituting marriage in Paradise, He said to our first parents, and through them to all future spouses: "Increase and multiply, and fill the earth."[13] As St. Augustine admirably deduces from the words of the holy Apostle Saint Paul to Timothy[14] when he says: "The Apostle himself is therefore a witness that marriage is for the sake of generation: 'I wish,' he says, 'young girls to marry.' And, as if someone said to him, 'Why?,' he immediately adds: 'To bear children, to be mothers of families.'"[15]

12. How great a boon of God this is, and how great a blessing of matrimony is clear from a consideration of man's dignity and of his sublime end. For man surpasses all other visible creatures by the superiority of his rational nature alone. Besides, God wishes men to be born not only that they should live and fill the earth, but much more that they may be worshippers of God, that they may know Him and love Him and finally enjoy Him for ever in heaven; and this end, since man is raised by

---

13   *Gen.*, I, 28.
14   *I Tim.*, V, 14.
15   St. August., *De bono coniug.*, cap. 24 n. 32.

God in a marvelous way to the supernatural order, surpasses all that eye hath seen, and ear heard, and all that hath entered into the heart of man.[16] From which it is easily seen how great a gift of divine goodness and how remarkable a fruit of marriage are children born by the omnipotent power of God through the cooperation of those bound in wedlock.

13. But Christian parents must also understand that they are destined not only to propagate and preserve the human race on earth, indeed not only to educate any kind of worshippers of the true God, but children who are to become members of the Church of Christ, to raise up fellow-citizens of the Saints, and members of God's household,[17] that the worshippers of God and Our Savior may daily increase.

14. For although Christian spouses even if sanctified themselves cannot transmit sanctification to their progeny, nay, although the very natural process of generating life has become the way of death by which original sin is passed on to posterity, nevertheless, they share to some extent in the blessings of that primeval marriage of Paradise, since it is theirs to offer their offspring to the Church in order that by this most fruitful Mother of the children of God they may be regenerated through the laver of Baptism unto supernatural justice

16 I *Cor.*, II, 9
17 *Eph.*, II, 19.

and finally be made living members of Christ, partakers of immortal life, and heirs of that eternal glory to which we all aspire from our inmost heart.

15. If a true Christian mother weigh well these things, she will indeed understand with a sense of deep consolation that of her the words of Our Savior were spoken: "A woman ... when she hath brought forth the child remembereth no more the anguish, for joy that a man is born into the world";[18] and proving herself superior to all the pains and cares and solicitudes of her maternal office with a more just and holy joy than that of the Roman matron, the mother of the Gracchi, she will rejoice in the Lord crowned as it were with the glory of her offspring. Both husband and wife, however, receiving these children with joy and gratitude from the hand of God, will regard them as a talent committed to their charge by God, not only to be employed for their own advantage or for that of an earthly commonwealth, but to be restored to God with interest on the day of reckoning.

16. The blessing of offspring, however, is not completed by the mere begetting of them, but something else must be added, namely the proper education of the offspring. For the most wise God would have failed to make sufficient provision for children that had been

18   John, XVI, 21.

born, and so for the whole human race, if He had not given to those to whom He had entrusted the power and right to beget them, the power also and the right to educate them. For no one can fail to see that children are incapable of providing wholly for themselves, even in matters pertaining to their natural life, and much less in those pertaining to the supernatural, but require for many years to be helped, instructed, and educated by others. Now it is certain that both by the law of nature and of God this right and duty of educating their offspring belongs in the first place to those who began the work of nature by giving them birth, and they are indeed forbidden to leave unfinished this work and so expose it to certain ruin. But in matrimony provision has been made in the best possible way for this education of children that is so necessary, for, since the parents are bound together by an indissoluble bond, the care and mutual help of each is always at hand.

17. Since, however, We have spoken fully elsewhere on the Christian education of youth,[19] let Us sum it all up by quoting once more the words of St. Augustine: "As regards the offspring it is provided that they should be begotten lovingly and educated religiously,"[20] and this is also expressed succinctly in the Code of Canon Law: "The primary end of

19   Encycl. *Divini illius Magistri,* 31 Dec. 1929.
20   St. August., *De Gen. ad litt.,* lib. IX, cap. 7, n. 12.

marriage is the procreation and the education of children."[21]

18. Nor must We omit to remark, in fine, that since the duty entrusted to parents for the good of their children is of such high dignity and of such great importance, every use of the faculty given by God for the procreation of new life is the right and the privilege of the married state alone, by the law of God and of nature, and must be confined absolutely within the sacred limits of that state.

The Blessing of Fidelity

19. The second blessing of matrimony which We said was mentioned by St. Augustine, is the blessing of conjugal honor which consists in the mutual fidelity of the spouses in fulfilling the marriage contract, so that what belongs to one of the parties by reason of this contract sanctioned by divine law, may not be denied to him or permitted to any third person; nor may there be conceded to one of the parties anything which, being contrary to the rights and laws of God and entirely opposed to matrimonial faith, can never be conceded.

20. Wherefore, conjugal faith, or honor, demands in the first place the complete unity of matrimony which the Creator Himself laid down in the beginning when He wished it

---

21 *Cod. iur. can.*, c. 1013 & 7.

to be not otherwise than between one man and one woman. And although afterwards this primeval law was relaxed to some extent by God, the Supreme Legislator, there is no doubt that the law of the Gospel fully restored that original and perfect unity, and abrogated all dispensations, as the words of Christ and the constant teaching and action of the Church show plainly. With reason, therefore, does the Sacred Council of Trent solemnly declare: "Christ Our Lord very clearly taught that in this bond two persons only are to be united and joined together when He said: 'Therefore they are no longer two, but one flesh.'"[22]

21. Nor did Christ Our Lord wish only to condemn any form of polygamy or polyandry, as they are called, whether successive or simultaneous, and every other external dishonorable act, but, in order that the sacred bonds of marriage may be guarded absolutely inviolate, He forbade also even willful thoughts and desires of such like things: "But I say to you, that whosoever shall look on a woman to lust after her hath already committed adultery with her in his heart."[23] Which words of Christ Our Lord cannot be annulled even by the consent of one of the partners of marriage for they express a law of God and of nature which no will of man can break or bend.[24]

---

22 Conc. Trid., Sess. XXIV.
23 Matth., V, 28.
24 *Decr. S. Officii,* 2 March 1679, propos. 50.

22. Nay, that mutual familiar association between the spouses themselves, if the blessing of conjugal faith is to shine with becoming splendor, must be distinguished by chastity so that husband and wife bear themselves in all things with the law of God and of nature, and endeavor always to follow the will of their most wise and holy Creator with the greatest reverence toward the work of God.

23. This conjugal faith, however, which is most aptly called by St. Augustine the "faith of chastity," blooms more freely, more beautifully and more nobly, when it is rooted in that more excellent soil, the love of husband and wife which pervades all the duties of married life and holds pride of place in Christian marriage. For matrimonial faith demands that husband and wife be joined in an especially holy and pure love, not as adulterers love each other, but as Christ loved the Church. This precept the Apostle laid down when he said: "Husbands, love your wives as Christ also loved the Church,"[25] that Church which of a truth He embraced with a boundless love not for the sake of His own advantage, but seeking only the good of His Spouse.[26] The love, then, of which We are speaking is not that based on the passing lust of the moment nor does it consist in pleasing words only, but in the deep attachment of the heart which is

25 *Eph.*, V, 25; Col., III, 19.
26 *Catech. Rom.*, II, cap. VIII q. 24.

expressed in action, since love is proved by deeds.[27] This outward expression of love in the home demands not only mutual help but must go further; must have as its primary purpose that man and wife help each other day by day in forming and perfecting themselves in the interior life, so that through their partnership in life they may advance ever more and more in virtue, and above all that they may grow in true love toward God and their neighbor, on which indeed "dependeth the whole Law and the Prophets."[28] For all men of every condition, in whatever honorable walk of life they may be, can and ought to imitate that most perfect example of holiness placed before man by God, namely Christ Our Lord, and by God's grace to arrive at the summit of perfection, as is proved by the example set us of many saints.

24. This mutual molding of husband and wife, this determined effort to perfect each other, can in a very real sense, as the Roman Catechism teaches, be said to be the chief reason and purpose of matrimony, provided matrimony be looked at not in the restricted sense as instituted for the proper conception and education of the child, but more widely as the blending of life as a whole and the mutual interchange and sharing thereof.

---

27   St. Gregory the Great, *Hom. XXX in Evang.* (John XIV,23–31), n.1.
28   Matth., XXII, 40.

25. By this same love it is necessary that all the other rights and duties of the marriage state be regulated, as the words of the Apostle — "Let the husband render the debt to the wife, and the wife also in like manner to the husband"[29] — express not only a law of justice but also one of charity.

26. Domestic society being confirmed, therefore, by this bond of love, there should flourish in it that "order of love," as St. Augustine calls it. This order includes both the primacy of the husband with regard to the wife and children, and the ready subjection of the wife and her willing obedience, which the Apostle commends in these words: "Let women be subject to their husbands as to the Lord, because the husband is the head of the wife, and Christ is the head of the Church."[30]

27. This subjection, however, does not deny or take away the liberty which fully belongs to the woman both in view of her dignity as a human person, and in view of her most noble office as wife and mother and companion; nor does it bid her obey her husband's every request if not in harmony with right reason or with the dignity due to a wife; nor, in fine, does it imply that the wife should be put on a level with those persons who in law are called minors, to whom it is not customary to allow free exercise of their

29   I *Cor.*, VII, 3.
30   *Eph.*, V, 22–23.

rights on account of their lack of mature judgment, or of their ignorance of human affairs. But it forbids that exaggerated liberty which cares not for the good of the family; it forbids that in this body which is the family, the heart be separated from the head to the great detriment of the whole body and the proximate danger of ruin. For if the man is the head, the woman is the heart, and as he occupies the chief place in ruling, so she may and ought to claim for herself the chief place in love.

28. Again, this subjection of wife to husband in its degree and manner may vary according to the different conditions of persons, place and time. In fact, if the husband neglects his duty, it falls to the wife to take his place in directing the family. But the structure of the family and its fundamental law, established and confirmed by God, must always and everywhere be maintained intact.

29. With great wisdom Our predecessor Leo XIII, of happy memory, in the Encyclical on Christian marriage which We have already mentioned, speaking of this order to be maintained between man and wife, teaches: "The man is the ruler of the family, and the head of the woman; but because she is flesh of his flesh and bone of his bone, let her be subject and obedient to the man, not as a servant but as a companion, so that nothing be lacking of honor or of dignity in the obedience which

she pays. Let divine charity be the constant guide of their mutual relations, both in him who rules and in her who obeys, since each bears the image, the one of Christ, the other of the Church."[31]

30. These, then, are the elements which compose the blessing of conjugal faith: unity, chastity, charity, honorable noble obedience, which are at the same time an enumeration of the benefits which are bestowed on husband and wife in their married state, benefits by which the peace, the dignity and the happiness of matrimony are securely preserved and fostered. Wherefore it is not surprising that this conjugal faith has always been counted amongst the most priceless and special blessings of matrimony.

The Blessing of Sacrament

31. But this accumulation of benefits is completed and, as it were, crowned by that blessing of Christian marriage which in the words of St. Augustine we have called the sacrament, by which is denoted both the indissolubility of the bond and the raising and hallowing of the contract by Christ Himself, whereby He made it an efficacious sign of grace.

32. In the first place Christ Himself lays stress on the indissolubility and firmness of

---

31   Encycl. *Arcanum divinae sapientiae*, 10 Febr. 1880.

the marriage bond when He says: "What God hath joined together let no man put asunder,"[32] and: "Everyone that putteth away his wife and marrieth another committeth adultery, and he that marrieth her that is put away from her husband committeth adultery."[33]

33. And St. Augustine clearly places what he calls the blessing of matrimony in this indissolubility when he says: "In the sacrament it is provided that the marriage bond should not be broken, and that a husband or wife, if separated, should not be joined to another even for the sake of offspring."[34]

34. And this inviolable stability, although not in the same perfect measure in every case, belongs to every true marriage, for the word of the Lord: "What God hath joined together let no man put asunder," must of necessity include all true marriages without exception, since it was spoken of the marriage of our first parents, the prototype of every future marriage. Therefore although before Christ the sublimeness and the severity of the primeval law was so tempered that Moses permitted to the chosen people of God on account of the hardness of their hearts that a bill of divorce might be given in certain circumstances, nevertheless, Christ, by virtue of His supreme

---

32   Matth., XIX, 6.
33   Luke, XVI, 18.
34   St. August., *De Gen. ad litt.* lib. IX, cap. 7, n. 12.

legislative power, revoked this concession of greater liberty and restored the primeval law in its integrity by those words which must never be forgotten, "What God hath joined together let no man put asunder." Wherefore, Our predecessor Pius VI of happy memory, writing to the Bishop of Agria, most wisely said: "Hence it is clear that marriage even in the state of nature, and certainly long before it was raised to the dignity of a sacrament, was divinely instituted in such a way that it should carry with it a perpetual and indissoluble bond which cannot therefore be dissolved by any civil law. Therefore although the sacramental element may be absent from a marriage as is the case among unbelievers, still in such a marriage, inasmuch as it is a true marriage, there must remain and indeed there does remain that perpetual bond which by divine right is so bound up with matrimony from its first institution that it is not subject to any civil power. And so, whatever marriage is said to be contracted, either it is so contracted that it is really a true marriage, in which case it carries with it that enduring bond which by divine right is inherent in every true marriage; or it is thought to be contracted without that perpetual bond, and in that case there is no marriage, but an illicit union opposed of its very nature to the divine law, which therefore cannot be entered into or maintained."[35]

---

35   Pius VI, *Rescript. ad Episc. Agriens.*, 11 July 1789.

35. And if this stability seems to be open to exception, however rare the exception may be, as in the case of certain natural marriages between unbelievers, or amongst Christians in the case of those marriages which though valid have not been consummated [*ratum tantum*], that exception does not depend on the will of men nor on that of any merely human power, but on divine law, of which the only guardian and interpreter is the Church of Christ. However, not even this power can ever affect for any cause whatsoever a Christian marriage which is valid and has been consummated [*ratum et consummatum*], for as it is plain that here the marriage contract has its full completion, so, by the will of God, there is also the greatest firmness and indissolubility which may not be destroyed by any human authority.

36. If we wish with all reverence to inquire into the intimate reason of this divine decree, Venerable Brethren, we shall easily see it in the mystical signification of Christian marriage which is fully and perfectly verified in consummated marriage between Christians. For, as the Apostle says in his Epistle to the Ephesians,[36] the marriage of Christians recalls that most perfect union which exists between Christ and the Church: "Sacramentum hoc magnum est, ego autem dico, in Christo et in ecclesia" — which union, as long as Christ

36 *Eph.*, V, 32.

shall live and the Church through Him, can never be dissolved by any separation. And this St. Augustine clearly declares in these words: "This is safeguarded in Christ and the Church, which, living with Christ who lives for ever may never be divorced from Him. The observance of this sacrament is such in the City of God ... that is, in the Church of Christ, that when for the sake of begetting children, women marry or are taken to wife, it is wrong to leave a wife that is sterile in order to take another by whom children may be had. Anyone doing this is guilty of adultery, just as if he married another – guilty not by the law of the day, according to which when one's partner is put away another may be taken, which the Lord allowed in the law of Moses because of the hardness of the hearts of the people of Israel; but by the law of the Gospel."[37]

37. Indeed, how many and how important are the benefits which flow from the indissolubility of matrimony cannot escape anyone who gives even a brief consideration either to the good of the married parties and the offspring or to the welfare of human society. First of all, both husband and wife possess a positive guarantee of the endurance of this stability which that generous yielding of their persons and the intimate fellowship of their hearts by their nature strongly require, since true

---

37   St. August., *De nupt. et concup.*, lib. I, cap. 10.

love never falls away.[38] Besides, a strong bulwark is set up in defense of a loyal chastity against incitements to infidelity, should any be encountered either from within or from without; any anxious fear lest in adversity or old age the other spouse would prove unfaithful is precluded and in its place there reigns a calm sense of security. Moreover, the dignity of both man and wife is maintained and mutual aid is most satisfactorily assured, while through the indissoluble bond, always enduring, the spouses are warned continuously that not for the sake of perishable things nor that they may serve their passions, but that they may procure one for the other high and lasting good have they entered into the nuptial partnership, to be dissolved only by death. In the training and education of children, which must extend over a period of many years, it plays a great part, since the grave and long enduring burdens of this office are best borne by the united efforts of the parents. Nor do lesser benefits accrue to human society as a whole. For experience has taught that unassailable stability in matrimony is a fruitful source of virtuous life and of habits of integrity. Where this order of things obtains, the happiness and well being of the nation is safely guarded; what the families and individuals are, so also is the State, for a body is determined by its parts. Wherefore,

---

38   I *Cor.*, XIII, 8.

both for the private good of husband, wife and children, as likewise for the public good of human society, they indeed deserve well who strenuously defend the inviolable stability of matrimony.

38. But considering the benefits of the Sacrament, besides the firmness and indissolubility, there are also much higher emoluments as the word "sacrament" itself very aptly indicates; for to Christians this is not a meaningless and empty name. Christ the Lord, the Institutor and Perfecter of the holy sacraments,[39] by raising the matrimony of His faithful to the dignity of a true sacrament of the New Law, made it a sign and source of that peculiar internal grace by which "it perfects natural love, confirms an indissoluble union, and sanctifies both man and wife."[40]

39. And since the valid matrimonial consent among the faithful was constituted by Christ as a sign of grace, the sacramental nature is so intimately bound up with Christian wedlock that there can be no true marriage between baptized persons "without it being by that very fact a sacrament."[41]

40. By the very fact, therefore, that the faithful with sincere mind give such consent, they open up for themselves a treasure

---

39   Conc. Trid., Sess. XXIV.
40   Conc. Trid., Sess. XXIV.
41   *Cod. iur. can.,* c. 1012.

of sacramental grace from which they draw supernatural power for the fulfilling of their rights and duties faithfully, holily, perseveringly even unto death. Hence this sacrament not only increases sanctifying grace, the permanent principle of the supernatural life, in those who, as the expression is, place no obstacle in its way, but also adds particular gifts, dispositions, seeds of grace, by elevating and perfecting the natural powers. By these gifts the parties are assisted not only in understanding, but in knowing intimately, in adhering to firmly, in willing effectively, and in successfully putting into practice, those things which pertain to the marriage state, its aims and duties, giving them (*in fine*) right to the actual assistance of grace, whensoever they need it for fulfilling the duties of their state.

41. Nevertheless, since it is a law of divine Providence in the supernatural order that men do not reap the full fruit of the Sacraments which they receive after acquiring the use of reason unless they cooperate with grace, the grace of matrimony will remain for the most part an unused talent hidden in the field unless the parties exercise these supernatural powers and cultivate and develop the seeds of grace they have received. If, however, doing all that lies with their power, they cooperate diligently, they will be able with ease to bear the burdens of their state and to fulfill their duties. By such a sacrament they will

41

be strengthened, sanctified and in a manner consecrated. For, as St. Augustine teaches, just as by Baptism and Holy Orders a man is set aside and assisted either for the duties of Christian life or for the priestly office and is never deprived of their sacramental aid, almost in the same way (although not by a sacramental character), the faithful once joined by marriage ties can never be deprived of the help and the binding force of the sacrament. Indeed, as the Holy Doctor adds, even those who commit adultery carry with them that sacred yoke, although in this case not as a title to the glory of grace but for the ignominy of their guilty action, "as the soul by apostasy, withdrawing as it were from marriage with Christ, even though it may have lost its faith, does not lose the sacrament of Faith which it received at the laver of regeneration."[42]

42. These parties, let it be noted, not fettered but adorned by the golden bond of the sacrament, not hampered but assisted, should strive with all their might to the end that their wedlock, not only through the power and symbolism of the sacrament, but also through their spirit and manner of life, may be and remain always the living image of that most fruitful union of Christ with the Church, which is to be venerated as the sacred token of most perfect love.

---

42   St. August., *De nupt. et concup.*, lib. I, cap. 10.

43. All of these things, Venerable Brethren, you must consider carefully and ponder over with a lively faith if you would see in their true light the extraordinary benefits of matrimony—offspring, conjugal faith, and the sacrament. No one can fail to admire the divine Wisdom, Holiness and Goodness which, while respecting the dignity and happiness of husband and wife, has provided so bountifully for the conservation and propagation of the human race by a single chaste and sacred fellowship of nuptial union.

II. ERRORS AND EVILS UNDERMINING MARRIAGE

44. When we consider the great excellence of chaste wedlock, Venerable Brethren, it appears all the more regrettable that particularly in our day we should witness this divine institution often scorned and on every side degraded.

45. For now, alas, not secretly nor under cover, but openly, with all sense of shame put aside, now by word, again by writings, by theatrical productions of every kind, by romantic fiction, by amorous and frivolous novels, by cinematographs portraying in vivid scene, in addresses broadcast by radio telephony, in short by all the inventions of modern science, the sanctity of marriage is trampled upon and derided; divorce, adultery, all the basest vices either are extolled or at least are depicted in such colors as to appear to be free of all reproach and infamy. Books are not lacking which dare to pronounce themselves as scientific but which in truth are merely coated with a veneer of science in order that they may the more easily insinuate their ideas. The doctrines defended in these are offered for sale as the productions of modern genius, of that genius namely, which, anxious only for truth, is considered to have *emancipated* itself from all those old-fashioned and immature opinions of the ancients; and to the number of these antiquated opinions they relegate the traditional doctrine of Christian marriage.

46. These thoughts are instilled into men of every class, rich and poor, masters and workers, lettered and unlettered, married and single, the godly and godless, old and young, but for these last, as easiest prey, the worst snares are laid.

47. Not all the sponsors of these new doctrines are carried to the extremes of unbridled lust; there are those who, striving as it were to ride a middle course, believe nevertheless that something should be conceded in our times as regards certain precepts of the divine and natural law. But these likewise, more or less wittingly, are emissaries of the great enemy who is ever seeking to sow cockle among the wheat.[43] We, therefore, whom the Father has appointed over His field, We who are bound by

---

43   Matth., XIII, 25.

Our most holy office to take care lest the good seed be choked by the weeds, believe it fitting to apply to Ourselves the most grave words of the Holy Ghost with which the Apostle Paul exhorted his beloved Timothy: "Be thou vigilant... Fulfill thy ministry... Preach the word, be instant in season, out of season, reprove, entreat, rebuke in all patience and doctrine."[44]

48. And in order that the deceits of the enemy may be avoided, it is necessary first of all that they be laid bare; since much is to be gained by denouncing these fallacies for the sake of the unwary, even though We prefer not to name these iniquities "as becometh saints,"[45] yet for the welfare of souls We cannot remain altogether silent.

49. To begin at the very source of these evils, their basic principle lies in this, that matrimony is repeatedly declared to be not instituted by the Author of nature nor raised by Christ the Lord to the dignity of a true sacrament, but invented by man. Some confidently assert that they have found no evidence of the existence of matrimony in nature or in her laws, but regard it merely as the means of producing life and of gratifying in one way or another a vehement impulse; on the other hand, others recognize that certain beginnings or, as it were, seeds of true wedlock are found

44   II *Tim.*, IV, 2–5.
45   *Eph.*, V, 3.

in the nature of man since, unless men were bound together by some form of permanent tie, the dignity of husband and wife or the natural end of propagating and rearing the offspring would not receive satisfactory provision. At the same time they maintain that in all beyond this germinal idea matrimony, through various concurrent causes, is invented solely by the mind of man, established solely by his will.

50. How grievously all these err and how shamelessly they leave the ways of honesty is already evident from what we have set forth here regarding the origin and nature of wedlock, its purposes and the good inherent in it. The evil of this teaching is plainly seen from the consequences which its advocates deduce from it, namely, that the laws, institutions and customs by which wedlock is governed, since they take their origin solely from the will of man, are subject entirely to him, hence can and must be founded, changed and abrogated according to human caprice and the shifting circumstances of human affairs; that the generative power which is grounded in nature itself is more sacred and has wider range than matrimony—hence it may be exercised both outside as well as within the confines of wedlock, and even where the purpose of matrimony be set aside, as though to suggest that the license of a base fornicating woman should enjoy the same rights as the chaste motherhood of a lawfully wedded wife.

51. Armed with these principles, some men go so far as to concoct new species of unions, suited, as they say, to the present temper of men and the times, which various new forms of matrimony they presume to label "temporary," "experimental," and "companionate." These offer all the indulgence of matrimony and its rights without, however, the indissoluble bond, and without offspring, unless later the parties alter their cohabitation into a matrimony in the full sense of the law.

52. Indeed there are some who desire and insist that these practices be legitimatized by the law or, at least, excused by their general acceptance among the people. They do not seem even to suspect that these proposals partake of nothing of the modern "culture" in which they glory so much, but are simply hateful abominations which beyond all question reduce our truly cultured nations to the barbarous standards of savage peoples.

Errors Regarding Offspring

53. And now, Venerable Brethren, we shall explain in detail the evils opposed to each of the benefits of matrimony. First consideration is due to the offspring, which many have the boldness to call the disagreeable burden of matrimony and which they say is to be carefully avoided by married people not through virtuous continence (which Christian

law permits in matrimony when both parties consent) but by frustrating the marriage act. Some justify this criminal abuse on the ground that they are weary of children and wish to gratify their desires without their consequent burden. Others say that they cannot on the one hand remain continent nor on the other can they have children because of the difficulties whether on the part of the mother or on the part of family circumstances.

54. But no reason, however grave, may be put forward by which anything intrinsically against nature may become conformable to nature and morally good. Since, therefore, the conjugal act is destined primarily by nature for the begetting of children, those who in exercising it deliberately frustrate its natural power and purpose sin against nature and commit a deed which is shameful and intrinsically vicious.

55. Small wonder, therefore, if Holy Scripture bears witness that the Divine Majesty regards with greatest detestation this horrible crime and at times has punished it with death. As St. Augustine notes, "Intercourse even with one's legitimate wife is unlawful and wicked where the conception of the offspring is prevented. Onan, the son of Judah, did this and the Lord killed him for it."[46]

---

46   St. August., *De coniug. adult.*, lib. II, n. 12, *Gen*, XXXVIII, 8–10.

56. Since, therefore, openly departing from the uninterrupted Christian tradition some recently have judged it possible solemnly to declare another doctrine regarding this question, the Catholic Church, to whom God has entrusted the defense of the integrity and purity of morals, standing upright in the midst of the moral ruin which surrounds her, in order that she may preserve the chastity of the nuptial union from being defiled by this foul stain, raises her voice in token of her divine ambassadorship and through Our mouth proclaims anew: any use whatsoever of matrimony exercised in such a way that the act is deliberately frustrated in its natural power to generate life is an offense against the law of God and of nature, and those who indulge in such are branded with the guilt of a grave sin.[47]

57. We admonish, therefore, priests who hear confessions and others who have the care of

---

47 [The "some" to which the Pope refers at the start of this paragraph are the Anglican bishops who, at the Seventh Lambeth Conference in 1930, approved in a limited way the use of birth control. Prior to this decision, all mainstream Protestant denominations had assumed or defended the historic Christian teaching against contraception, but it was not long after Lambeth that Protestant denominations began to abandon this and many other traditional teachings in the area of sexual morality, which today are maintained either principally or even exclusively by the Catholic Church. The present paragraph anticipates the judgment given, with a fuller explanation, by Pope Paul VI in the encyclical letter *Humanae Vitae* of 1968.]

souls, in virtue of Our supreme authority and in Our solicitude for the salvation of souls, not to allow the faithful entrusted to them to err regarding this most grave law of God; much more, that they keep themselves immune from such false opinions, in no way conniving in them. If any confessor or pastor of souls, which may God forbid, lead the faithful entrusted to him into these errors or should at least confirm them by approval or by guilty silence, let him be mindful of the fact that he must render a strict account to God, the Supreme Judge, for the betrayal of his sacred trust, and let him take to himself the words of Christ: "They are blind and leaders of the blind: and if the blind lead the blind, both fall into the pit."[48]

58. As regards the evil use of matrimony, to pass over the arguments which are shameful, not infrequently others that are false and exaggerated are put forward. Holy Mother Church very well understands and clearly appreciates all that is said regarding the health of the mother and the danger to her life. And who would not grieve to think of these things? Who is not filled with the greatest admiration when he sees a mother risking her life with heroic fortitude, that she may preserve the life of the offspring which she has conceived? God alone, all bountiful and all merciful as He is, can reward her for the fulfillment of the office

---

48   Matth., XV, 14.

allotted to her by nature, and will assuredly repay her in a measure full to overflowing.[49]

59. Holy Church knows well that not infrequently one of the parties is sinned against rather than sinning, when for a grave cause he or she reluctantly allows the perversion of the right order. In such a case, there is no sin, provided that, mindful of the law of charity, he or she does not neglect to seek to dissuade and to deter the partner from sin. Nor are those considered as acting against nature who in the married state use their right in the proper manner although on account of natural reasons either of time or of certain defects, new life cannot be brought forth. For in matrimony as well as in the use of the matrimonial rights there are also secondary ends, such as mutual aid, the cultivating of mutual love, and the quieting of concupiscence which husband and wife are not forbidden to consider so long as they are subordinated to the primary end and so long as the intrinsic nature of the act is preserved.

60. We are deeply touched by the sufferings of those parents who, in extreme want, experience great difficulty in rearing their children.

61. However, they should take care lest the calamitous state of their external affairs should be the occasion for a much more calamitous error. No difficulty can arise that justifies the

---

49   Luke, VI, 38.

putting aside of the law of God which forbids all acts intrinsically evil. There is no possible circumstance in which husband and wife cannot, strengthened by the grace of God, fulfill faithfully their duties and preserve in wedlock their chastity unspotted. This truth of Christian Faith is expressed by the teaching of the Council of Trent. "Let no one be so rash as to assert that which the Fathers of the Council have placed under anathema, namely, that there are precepts of God impossible for the just to observe. God does not ask the impossible, but by His commands, instructs you to do what you are able, and to pray for what you are not able that He may help you."[50]

62. This same doctrine was again solemnly repeated and confirmed by the Church in the condemnation of the Jansenist heresy which dared to utter this blasphemy against the goodness of God: "Some precepts of God are, when one considers the powers which man possesses, impossible of fulfillment even to the just who wish to keep the law and strive to do so; grace is lacking whereby these laws could be fulfilled."[51]

63. But another very grave crime is to be noted, Venerable Brethren, which regards the taking of the life of the offspring hidden in the mother's womb. Some wish it to be

50   Conc. Trid., Sess. VI, cap. 11.
51   Const. Apost. *Cum occasione,* 31 May 1653, prop. 1.

52

allowed and left to the will of the father or the mother; others say it is unlawful unless there are weighty reasons which they call by the name of medical, social, or eugenic "indication." Because this matter falls under the penal laws of the state by which the destruction of the offspring begotten but unborn is forbidden, these people demand that the "indication," which in one form or another they defend, be recognized as such by the public law and in no way penalized. There are those, moreover, who ask that the public authorities provide aid for these death-dealing operations, a thing which, sad to say, everyone knows is of very frequent occurrence in some places.

64. As to the "medical and therapeutic indication" to which, using their own words, we have made reference, Venerable Brethren, however much we may pity the mother whose health and even life is gravely imperiled in the performance of the duty allotted to her by nature, nevertheless what could ever be a sufficient reason for excusing in any way the direct murder of the innocent? This is precisely what we are dealing with here. Whether inflicted upon the mother or upon the child, it is against the precept of God and the law of nature: "Thou shalt not kill."[52] The life of each is equally sacred, and no one has the power, not even the public authority, to destroy it. It

---

52   *Exod.*, XX, 13; cfr. Decr. S. Offic. 4 May 1897, 24 July 1895; 31 May 1884.

is of no use to appeal to the right of taking away life for here it is a question of the innocent, whereas that right has regard only to the guilty; nor is there here question of defense by bloodshed against an unjust aggressor (for who would call an innocent child an unjust aggressor?); again there is not question here of what is called the "law of extreme necessity" which could even extend to the direct killing of the innocent. Upright and skillful doctors strive most praiseworthily to guard and preserve the lives of both mother and child; on the contrary, those show themselves most unworthy of the noble medical profession who encompass the death of one or the other, through a pretense at practicing medicine or through motives of misguided pity.

65. All of which agrees with the stern words of the Bishop of Hippo in denouncing those wicked parents who seek to remain childless, and failing in this, are not ashamed to put their offspring to death: "Sometimes this lustful cruelty or cruel lust goes so far as to seek to procure a baneful sterility, and if this fails the fetus conceived in the womb is in one way or another smothered or evacuated, in the desire to destroy the offspring before it has life, or if it already lives in the womb, to kill it before it is born. If both man and woman are party to such practices they are not spouses at all; and if from the first they have carried on thus they have come together

not for honest wedlock, but for impure gratification. If both are not party to these deeds, I make bold to say that either the one makes herself a mistress of the husband, or the other simply the paramour of his wife."[53]

66. What is asserted in favor of the social and eugenic "indication" may and must be accepted, provided lawful and upright methods are employed within the proper limits; but to wish to put forward reasons based upon them for the killing of the innocent is unthinkable and contrary to the divine precept promulgated in the words of the Apostle: Evil is not to be done that good may come of it.[54]

67. Those who hold the reins of government should not forget that it is the duty of public authority by appropriate laws and sanctions to defend the lives of the innocent, and this all the more so since those whose lives are endangered and assailed cannot defend themselves — among whom we must mention in the first place infants hidden in the mother's womb. And if the public magistrates not only do not defend them, but by their laws and ordinances betray them to death at the hands of doctors or of others, let them remember that God is the Judge and Avenger of innocent blood which cried from earth to Heaven.[55]

---

53   St. August., *De nupt. et concupisc.*, cap. XV.
54   *Rom.*, III, 8.
55   *Gen.*, IV, 10.

68. Finally, that pernicious practice must be condemned which closely touches upon the natural right of man to enter matrimony but affects also in a real way the welfare of the off-spring. For there are some who, over-solicitous for the cause of eugenics, not only give salutary counsel for more certainly procuring the strength and health of the future child – which, indeed, is not contrary to right reason – but put eugenics before aims of a higher order, and by public authority wish to prevent from marrying all those whom, even though naturally fit for marriage, they consider, according to the norms and conjectures of their investigations, would, through hereditary transmission, bring forth defective offspring. And more, they wish to legislate to deprive these of that natural faculty by medical action despite their unwillingness; and this they do not propose as an infliction of grave punishment under the authority of the state for a crime committed, nor to prevent future crimes by guilty persons, but against every right and good they wish the civil authority to arrogate to itself a power over a faculty which it never had and can never legitimately possess.

69. Those who act in this way are at fault in losing sight of the fact that the family is more sacred than the State and that men are begotten not for the earth and for time, but for Heaven and eternity. Although often these individuals are to be dissuaded from entering

into matrimony, certainly it is wrong to brand men with the stigma of crime because they contract marriage, on the ground that, despite the fact that they are in every respect capable of matrimony, they will give birth only to defective children, even though they use all care and diligence.

70. Public magistrates have no direct power over the bodies of their subjects; therefore, where no crime has taken place and there is no cause present for grave punishment, they can never directly harm or tamper with the integrity of the body, either for reasons of eugenics or for any other reason. St. Thomas teaches this when inquiring whether human judges for the sake of preventing future evils can inflict punishment. He admits that the power indeed exists as regards certain other forms of evil, but justly and properly denies it as regards the maiming of the body. "No one who is guiltless may be punished by a human tribunal either by flogging to death, or by mutilation, or by beating."[56]

71. Furthermore, Christian doctrine establishes, and the light of human reason makes it most clear, that private individuals have no other power over the members of their bodies than that which pertains to their natural ends; and they are not free to destroy or mutilate their members, or in any other way render

---

56 *Sum. theol.*, 2a 2ae, q. 108, a. 4, ad 2um.

themselves unfit for their natural functions, except when no other provision can be made for the good of the whole body.

Errors Regarding Fidelity

72. We may now consider another class of errors concerning conjugal faith. Every sin committed as regards the offspring becomes in some way a sin against conjugal faith, since both these blessings are essentially connected. However, we must mention briefly the sources of error and vice corresponding to those virtues which are demanded by conjugal faith, namely the chaste honor existing between man and wife, the due subjection of wife to husband, and the true love which binds both parties together.

73. It follows therefore that they are destroying mutual fidelity, who think that the ideas and morality of our present time concerning a certain harmful and false friendship with a third party can be countenanced, and who teach that a greater freedom of feeling and action in such external relations should be allowed to man and wife, particularly as many (so they consider) are possessed of an inborn sexual tendency which cannot be satisfied within the narrow limits of monogamous marriage. That rigid attitude which condemns all sensual affections and actions with a third party they imagine to be a narrowing of mind

and heart, something obsolete, or an abject form of jealousy, and as a result they look upon whatever penal laws are passed by the State for the preserving of conjugal faith as void or to be abolished. Such unworthy and idle opinions are condemned by that noble instinct which is found in every chaste husband and wife, and even by the light of the testimony of nature alone — a testimony that is sanctioned and confirmed by the command of God: "Thou shalt not commit adultery,"[57] and the words of Christ: "Whosoever shall look on a woman to lust after her hath already committed adultery with her in his heart."[58] The force of this divine precept can never be weakened by any merely human custom, bad example or pretext of human progress, for just as it is the one and the same "Jesus Christ, yesterday and today and the same for ever,"[59] so it is the one and the same doctrine of Christ that abides and of which no one jot or tittle shall pass away till all is fulfilled.[60]

74. The same false teachers who try to dim the luster of conjugal faith and purity do not scruple to do away with the honorable and trusting obedience which the woman owes to the man. Many of them even go further and assert that such a subjection of one party to the other is

---

57 *Exod.*, XX, 14.
58 Matth., V, 28.
59 *Hebr.*, XIII, 8.
60 Matth., V, 18.

unworthy of human dignity, that the rights of husband and wife are equal; wherefore, they boldly proclaim the emancipation of women has been or ought to be effected. This emancipation in their ideas must be threefold: in the ruling of the domestic society, in the administration of family affairs and in the rearing of the children. It must be social, economic, physiological: – physiological, that is to say, the woman is to be freed at her own good pleasure from the burdensome duties properly belonging to a wife as companion and mother (We have already said that this is not an emancipation but a crime); social, inasmuch as the wife being freed from the cares of children and family, should, to the neglect of these, be able to follow her own bent and devote herself to business and even public affairs; finally economic, whereby the woman even without the knowledge and against the wish of her husband may be at liberty to conduct and administer her own affairs, giving her attention chiefly to these rather than to children, husband and family.

75. This, however, is not the true emancipation of woman, nor that rational and exalted liberty which belongs to the noble office of a Christian woman and wife; it is rather the debasing of the womanly character and the dignity of motherhood, and indeed of the whole family, as a result of which the husband suffers the loss of his wife, the children of their mother, and the home and the whole family of an ever

watchful guardian. More than this, this false liberty and unnatural equality with the husband is to the detriment of the woman herself, for if the woman descends from her truly regal throne to which she has been raised within the walls of the home by means of the Gospel, she will soon be reduced to the old state of slavery (if not in appearance, certainly in reality) and become, as amongst the pagans, the mere instrument of man.

76. This equality of rights which is so much exaggerated and distorted, must indeed be recognized in those rights which belong to the dignity of the human soul and which are proper to the marriage contract and inseparably bound up with wedlock. In such things undoubtedly both parties enjoy the same rights and are bound by the same obligations. In other things there must be a certain inequality and due accommodation, which is demanded by the good of the family and the right ordering and unity and stability of home life.

77. As, however, the social and economic conditions of the married woman must in some way be altered on account of changes in social relations, it is part of the office of the public authority to adapt the civil rights of the wife to modern needs and requirements, keeping in view what the natural disposition and temperament of the female sex, good morality, and the welfare of the family demand, and

provided always that the essential order of the domestic society remain intact, founded as it is on something higher than human authority and wisdom, namely on the authority and wisdom of God, and so not changeable by public laws or at the pleasure of private individuals.

78. These enemies of marriage go further, however, when they substitute for that true and solid love, which is the basis of conjugal happiness, a certain vague compatibility of temperament. This they call sympathy and assert that, since it is the only bond by which husband and wife are linked together, when it ceases the marriage is completely dissolved. What else is this than to build a house upon sand? — a house that in the words of Christ would forthwith be shaken and collapse, as soon as it was exposed to the waves of adversity: "and the winds blew and they beat upon that house, and it fell, and great was the fall thereof."[61] On the other hand, the house built upon a rock, that is to say on mutual conjugal chastity and strengthened by a deliberate and constant union of spirit, will not only never fall away but will never be shaken by adversity.

Errors Regarding Sacrament

79. We have so far, Venerable Brethren, shown the excellency of the first two blessings of

---

61   Matth., VII. 27.

Christian wedlock which the modern subverters of society are attacking. And now
considering that the third blessing, which is
that of the sacrament, far surpasses the other
two, we should not be surprised to find that
this, because of its outstanding excellence, is
much more sharply attacked by the same people. They put forward in the first place that
matrimony belongs entirely to the profane
and purely civil sphere, that it is not to be
committed to the religious society, the Church
of Christ, but to civil society alone. They then
add that the marriage contract is to be freed
from any indissoluble bond, and that separation and divorce are not only to be tolerated
but sanctioned by the law; from which it follows finally that, robbed of all its holiness,
matrimony should be enumerated amongst the
secular and civil institutions. The first point is
contained in their contention that the civil act
itself should stand for the marriage contract
(civil matrimony, as it is called), while the religious act is to be considered a mere addition,
or at most a concession to a too superstitious
people. Moreover they want it to be no cause
for reproach that marriages be contracted by
Catholics with non-Catholics without any reference to religion or recourse to the ecclesiastical authorities. The second point which is
but a consequence of the first is to be found in
their excuse for complete divorce and in their
praise and encouragement of those civil laws

which favor the loosening of the bond itself. As the salient features of the religious character of all marriage and particularly of the sacramental marriage of Christians have been treated at length and supported by weighty arguments in the encyclical letters of Leo XIII, letters which We have frequently recalled to mind and expressly made our own, We refer you to them, repeating here only a few points.

80. Even by the light of reason alone and particularly if the ancient records of history are investigated, if the unwavering popular conscience is interrogated and the manners and institutions of all races examined, it is sufficiently obvious that there is a certain sacredness and religious character attaching even to the purely natural union of man and woman, "not something added by chance but innate, not imposed by men but involved in the nature of things," since it has "God for its author and has been even from the beginning a foreshadowing of the Incarnation of the Word of God."[62] This sacredness of marriage which is intimately connected with religion and all that is holy, arises from the divine origin we have just mentioned, from its purpose which is the begetting and education of children for God, and the binding of man and wife to God through Christian love and mutual support; and finally it arises from the

---

62   Leo XIII, Encycl. *Arcanum*, 10 Febr. 1880.

very nature of wedlock, whose institution is to be sought for in the farseeing Providence of God, whereby it is the means of transmitting life, thus making the parents the ministers, as it were, of the Divine Omnipotence. To this must be added that new element of dignity which comes from the sacrament, by which the Christian marriage is so ennobled and raised to such a level, that it appeared to the Apostle as a great sacrament, honorable in every way.[63]

81. This religious character of marriage, its sublime signification of grace and the union between Christ and the Church, evidently requires that those about to marry should show a holy reverence towards it, and zealously endeavor to make their marriage approach as nearly as possible to the archetype of Christ and the Church.

82. They, therefore, who rashly and heedlessly contract mixed marriages, from which the maternal love and providence of the Church dissuades her children for very sound reasons, fail conspicuously in this respect, sometimes with danger to their eternal salvation. This attitude of the Church to mixed marriages appears in many of her documents, all of which are summed up in the Code of Canon Law: "Everywhere and with the greatest strictness the Church forbids marriages between

---

63 *Eph.*, V, 32: *Hebr.* XIII, 4.

baptized persons, one of whom is a Catholic and the other a member of a schismatic or heretical sect; and if there is, added to this, the danger of the falling away of the Catholic party and the perversion of the children, such a marriage is forbidden also by the divine law."[64] If the Church occasionally on account of circumstances does not refuse to grant a dispensation from these strict laws (provided that the divine law remains intact and the dangers above mentioned are provided against by suitable safeguards), it is unlikely that the Catholic party will not suffer some detriment from such a marriage.

83. Whence it comes about not infrequently, as experience shows, that deplorable defections from religion occur among the offspring, or at least a headlong descent into that religious indifference which is closely allied to impiety. There is this also to be considered, that in these mixed marriages it becomes much more difficult to imitate by a lively conformity of spirit the mystery of which We have spoken, namely that close union between Christ and His Church.

84. Assuredly, also, will there be wanting that close union of spirit which as it is the sign and mark of the Church of Christ, so also should be the sign of Christian wedlock, its glory and adornment. For, where there exists diversity

---

64   *Cod. iur. can.,* c. 1060.

of mind, truth and feeling, the bond of union of mind and heart is wont to be broken, or at least weakened. From this comes the danger lest the love of man and wife grow cold and the peace and happiness of family life, resting as it does on the union of hearts, be destroyed. Many centuries ago indeed, the old Roman law had proclaimed: "Marriages are the union of male and female, a sharing of life and the communication of divine and human rights."[65] But especially, as We have pointed out, Venerable Brethren, the daily increasing facility of divorce is an obstacle to the restoration of marriage to that state of perfection which the divine Redeemer willed it should possess.

85. The advocates of the neo-paganism of today have learned nothing from the sad state of affairs, but instead, day by day, more and more vehemently, they continue by legislation to attack the indissolubility of the marriage bond, proclaiming that the lawfulness of divorce must be recognized, and that the antiquated laws should give place to a new and more humane legislation. Many and varied are the grounds put forward for divorce, some arising from the wickedness and the guilt of the persons concerned, others arising from the circumstances of the case; the former they describe as subjective, the latter as objective;

---

65 Modestinus, *in Dig.* (Lib. XXIII, II: *De ritu nuptiarum*), lib. I, Regularum.

in a word, whatever might make married life hard or unpleasant. They strive to prove their contentions regarding these grounds for the divorce legislation they would bring about, by various arguments. Thus, in the first place, they maintain that it is for the good of either party that the one who is innocent should have the right to separate from the guilty, or that the guilty should be withdrawn from a union which is unpleasing to him and against his will. In the second place, they argue, the good of the child demands this, for it will be deprived of a proper education or the natural fruits of it, and will too easily be affected by the discords and shortcomings of the parents, and drawn from the path of virtue. And thirdly the common good of society requires that these marriages should be completely dissolved, which are now incapable of producing their natural results, and that legal reparations should be allowed when crimes are to be feared as the result of the common habitation and interaction of the parties. This last, they say, must be admitted to avoid the crimes being committed purposely with a view to obtaining the desired sentence of divorce for which the judge can legally loose the marriage bond, as also to prevent people from coming before the courts when it is obvious from the state of the case that they are lying and perjuring themselves – all of which brings the court and the lawful authority into contempt. Hence the civil laws, in their opinion, have

to be reformed to meet these new requirements, to suit the changes of the times and the
changes in men's opinions, civil institutions
and customs. Each of these reasons is considered by them as conclusive, so that all taken
together offer a clear proof of the necessity
of granting divorce in certain cases.

86. Others, taking a step further, simply state
that marriage, being a private contract, is, like
other private contracts, to be left to the consent and good pleasure of both parties, and
so can be dissolved for any reason whatsoever.

87. Opposed to all these reckless opinions,
Venerable Brethren, stands the unalterable
law of God, fully confirmed by Christ, a law
that can never be deprived of its force by the
decrees of men, the ideas of a people or the
will of any legislator: "What God hath joined
together, let no man put asunder."[66] And if
any man, acting contrary to this law, shall
have put asunder, his action is null and void,
and the consequence remains, as Christ Himself has explicitly confirmed: "Everyone that
putteth away his wife and marrieth another,
committeth adultery: and he that marrieth her
that is put away from her husband committeth
adultery."[67] Moreover, these words refer to
every kind of marriage, even that which is
natural and legitimate only; for, as has already

66   Matth., XIX, 6.
67   Luke, XVI, 18.

been observed, that indissolubility by which the loosening of the bond is once and for all removed from the whim of the parties and from every secular power, is a property of every true marriage.

88. Let that solemn pronouncement of the Council of Trent be recalled to mind in which, under the stigma of anathema, it condemned these errors: "If anyone should say that on account of heresy or the hardships of cohabitation or a deliberate abuse of one party by the other the marriage tie may be loosened, let him be anathema;"[68] and again: "If anyone should say that the Church errs in having taught or in teaching that, according to the teaching of the Gospel and the Apostles, the bond of marriage cannot be loosed because of the sin of adultery of either party; or that neither party, even though he be innocent, having given no cause for the sin of adultery, can contract another marriage during the lifetime of the other; and that he commits adultery who marries another after putting away his adulterous wife, and likewise that she commits adultery who puts away her husband and marries another: let him be anathema."[69]

89. If therefore the Church has not erred and does not err in teaching this, and consequently it is certain that the bond of marriage

---

68   Conc. Trid., Sess. XXIV, cap. 5
69   Conc. Trid., Sess. XXIV, cap. 7

cannot be loosed even on account of the sin of adultery, it is evident that all the other weaker excuses that can be, and are usually brought forward, are of no value whatsoever. And the objections brought against the firmness of the marriage bond are easily answered. For, in certain circumstances, imperfect separation of the parties is allowed, the bond not being severed. This separation, which the Church herself permits, and expressly mentions in her Canon Law in those canons which deal with the separation of the parties as to marital relationship and cohabitation, removes all the alleged inconveniences and dangers.[70] It will be for the sacred law and, to some extent, also the civil law, in so far as civil matters are affected, to lay down the grounds, the conditions, the method and precautions to be taken in a case of this kind in order to safeguard the education of the children and the well-being of the family, and to remove all those evils which threaten the married persons, the children and the State. Now all those arguments that are brought forward to prove the indissolubility of the marriage tie, arguments which have already been touched upon, can equally be applied to excluding not only the necessity of divorce, but even the power to grant it; while for all the advantages that can be put forward for the former, there can be adduced as many disadvantages and evils

70 *Cod. iur. can.,* c. 1128 sqq.

which are a formidable menace to the whole of human society.

90. To revert again to the expression of Our predecessor, it is hardly necessary to point out what an amount of good is involved in the absolute indissolubility of wedlock and what a train of evils follows upon divorce. Whenever the marriage bond remains intact, then we find marriages contracted with a sense of safety and security, while, when separations are considered and the dangers of divorce are present, the marriage contract itself becomes insecure, or at least gives ground for anxiety and surprises. On the one hand we see a wonderful strengthening of goodwill and cooperation in the daily life of husband and wife, while, on the other, both of these are miserably weakened by the presence of a facility for divorce. Here we have at a very opportune moment a source of help by which both parties are enabled to preserve their purity and loyalty; there we find harmful inducements to unfaithfulness. On this side we find the birth of children and their instruction and upbringing effectively promoted, many avenues of discord closed amongst families and relations, and the beginnings of rivalry and jealousy easily suppressed; on that, very great obstacles to the birth and rearing of children and their education, and many occasions of quarrels, and seeds of jealousy sown everywhere. Finally, but especially, the dignity and position of women in civil and domestic society

is reinstated by the former; while by the latter it is shamefully lowered and the danger is incurred "of their being considered outcasts, slaves of the lust of men."[71]

91. To conclude with the important words of Leo XIII, since the destruction of family life "and the loss of national wealth is brought about more by the corruption of morals than by anything else, it is easily seen that divorce, which is born of the perverted morals of a people, and leads, as experience shows, to vicious habits in public and private life, is particularly opposed to the well-being of the family and of the State. The serious nature of these evils will be the more clearly recognized, when we remember that, once divorce has been allowed, there will be no sufficient means of keeping it in check within any definite bounds. Great is the force of example, greater still that of lust; and with such incitements it cannot but happen that divorce and its consequent setting loose of the passions should spread daily and attack the souls of many like a contagious disease or a river bursting its banks and flooding the land."[72]

92. Thus, as we read in the same letter, "unless things change, the human family and State have every reason to fear lest they should

---

71   Leo XIII, Encycl. *Arcanum divinae sapientiae* 10 Febr. 1880.
72   Encycl. *Arcanum*, 10 Febr. 1880.

suffer absolute ruin."[73] All this was written fifty years ago, yet it is confirmed by the daily increasing corruption of morals and the unheard of degradation of the family in those lands where Communism reigns unchecked.

III. PASTORAL REMEDIES

93. Thus far, Venerable Brethren, We have admired with due reverence what the all-wise Creator and Redeemer of the human race has ordained with regard to human marriage; at the same time we have expressed Our grief that such a pious ordinance of the divine Goodness should today, and on every side, be frustrated and trampled upon by the passions, errors and vices of men.

94. It is then fitting that, with all fatherly solicitude, We should turn Our mind to seek out suitable remedies whereby those most detestable abuses which We have mentioned may be removed, and everywhere marriage may again be revered. To this end, it behooves Us, above all else, to call to mind that firmly established principle, esteemed alike in sound philosophy and sacred theology: namely, that whatever things have deviated from their right order, cannot be brought back to that original state which is in harmony with their nature except by a return to the divine plan

---

73   Encycl. *Arcanum,* 10 Febr. 1880.

which, as the Angelic Doctor teaches,[74] is the exemplar of all right order.

95. Wherefore, Our predecessor of happy memory, Leo XIII, attacked the doctrine of the naturalists in these words: "It is a divinely appointed law that whatsoever things are constituted by God, the Author of nature, these we find the more useful and salutary, the more they remain in their natural state, unimpaired and unchanged; inasmuch as God, the Creator of all things, intimately knows what is suited to the constitution and the preservation of each, and by his will and mind has so ordained all this that each may duly achieve its purpose. But if the boldness and wickedness of men change and disturb this order of things so providentially disposed, then, indeed, things so wonderfully ordained will begin to be injurious, or will cease to be beneficial, either because, in the change, they have lost their power to benefit, or because God Himself is thus pleased to draw down chastisement on the pride and presumption of men."[75]

96. In order, therefore, to restore due order in this matter of marriage, it is necessary that all should bear in mind what is the divine plan and strive to conform to it.

---

74   St. Thom. Aquin, *Sum. theolog.,* 1a 2ae, q. 91, a. 1–2 .
75   Encycl. *Arcanum divinae sapientiae,* 10 Febr. 1880.

97. Wherefore, since the chief obstacle to this study is the power of unbridled lust, which indeed is the most potent cause of sinning against the sacred laws of matrimony, and since man cannot hold in check his passions, unless he first subject himself to God, this must be his primary endeavor, in accordance with the plan divinely ordained. For it is a sacred ordinance that whoever shall have first subjected himself to God will, by the aid of divine grace, be glad to subject to himself his own passions and concupiscence; while he who is a rebel against God will, to his sorrow, experience within himself the violent rebellion of his worst passions.

98. And how wisely this has been decreed St. Augustine thus shows: "This indeed is fitting, that the lower be subject to the higher, so that he who would have subject to himself whatever is below him, should himself submit to whatever is above him. Acknowledge order, seek peace. Be thou subject to God, and thy flesh subject to thee. What more fitting! What more fair! Thou art subject to the higher and the lower is subject to thee. Do thou serve Him who made thee, so that that which was made for thee may serve thee. For we do not commend this order, namely, 'The flesh to thee and thou to God,' but 'Thou to God, and the flesh to thee.' If, however, thou despisest the subjection of thyself to God, thou shalt never bring about the subjection of the flesh

76

to thyself. If thou dost not obey the Lord, thou shalt be tormented by thy servant."[76] This right ordering on the part of God's wisdom is mentioned by the holy Doctor of the Gentiles, inspired by the Holy Spirit, for in speaking of those ancient philosophers who refused to adore and reverence Him whom they knew to be the Creator of the universe, he says: "Wherefore God gave them up to the desires of their heart, unto uncleanness, to dishonor their own bodies among themselves;" and again: "For this same God delivered them up to shameful affections."[77] And St. James says: "God resisteth the proud and giveth grace to the humble,"[78] without which grace, as the same Doctor of the Gentiles reminds us, man cannot subdue the rebellion of his flesh.[79]

99. Consequently, as the onslaughts of these uncontrolled passions cannot in any way be lessened, unless the spirit first shows a humble compliance of duty and reverence towards its Maker, it is above all and before all needful that those who are joined in the bond of sacred wedlock should be wholly imbued with a profound and genuine sense of duty towards God, which will shape their whole lives, and fill their minds and wills with a very deep reverence for the majesty of God.

---

76 St. August., *Enarrat.* in Ps. 143.
77 *Rom.* I, 24, 26.
78 James IV, 6.
79 Rom., VII, VIII.

100. Quite fittingly, therefore, and quite in accordance with the defined norm of Christian sentiment, do those pastors of souls act who, to prevent married people from failing in the observance of God's law, urge them to perform their duty and exercise their religion so that they should give themselves to God, continually ask for His divine assistance, frequent the sacraments, and always nourish and preserve a loyal and thoroughly sincere devotion to God.

Combating Naturalism and Rationalism

101. They are greatly deceived who having underestimated or neglected these means which rise above nature, think that they can induce men by the use and discovery of the natural sciences, such as those of biology, the science of heredity, and the like, to curb their carnal desires. We do not say this in order to belittle those natural means which are not dishonest; for God is the Author of nature as well as of grace, and He has disposed the good things of both orders for the beneficial use of men. The faithful, therefore, can and ought to be assisted also by natural means. But they are mistaken who think that these means are able to establish chastity in the nuptial union, or that they are more effective than supernatural grace.

102. This conformity of wedlock and moral conduct with the divine laws respective of marriage, without which its effective restoration cannot be brought about, supposes, however, that all can discern readily, with real certainty, and without any accompanying error, what those laws are. But everyone can see to how many fallacies an avenue would be opened up and how many errors would become mixed with the truth, if it were left solely to the light of reason of each to find it out, or if it were to be discovered by the private interpretation of the truth which is revealed. And if this is applicable to many other truths of the moral order, we must all the more pay attention to those things, which appertain to marriage where the inordinate desire for pleasure can attack frail human nature and easily deceive it and lead it astray; this is all the more true of the observance of the divine law, which demands sometimes hard and repeated sacrifices, for which, as experience points out, a weak man can find so many excuses for avoiding the fulfillment of the divine law.

103. On this account, in order that no falsification or corruption of the divine law but a true genuine knowledge of it may enlighten the minds of men and guide their conduct, it is necessary that a filial and humble obedience towards the Church should be combined with devotedness to God and the desire of submitting to Him. For Christ Himself made the Church the teacher of truth in those things also which concern the right regulation of moral conduct, even though some knowledge

of the same is not beyond human reason. For just as God, in the case of the natural truths of religion and morals, added revelation to the light of reason so that what is right and true, "in the present state also of the human race, may be known readily, with real certainty, without any admixture of error,"[80] so for the same purpose he has constituted the Church the guardian and the teacher of the whole of the truth concerning religion and moral conduct; to her therefore should the faithful show obedience and subject their minds and hearts so as to be kept unharmed and free from error and moral corruption, and so that they shall not deprive themselves of that assistance given by God with such liberal bounty, they ought to show this due obedience not only when the Church defines something with solemn judgment, but also, in proper proportion, when by the constitutions and decrees of the Holy See, opinions are proscribed and condemned as dangerous or distorted.[81]

104. Wherefore, let the faithful also be on their guard against the overrated independence of private judgment and that false autonomy of human reason. For it is quite foreign to everyone bearing the name of a Christian to trust his own mental powers with such pride as to agree only with those things which he can examine from their inner

---

80   Conc. Vat., Sess. III, cap. 2.
81   Conc. Vat., Sess. III, cap. 4; Cod. iur. can., c. 1324.

nature, and to imagine that the Church, sent by God to teach and guide all nations, is not conversant with present affairs and circumstances; or even that they must obey only in those matters which she has decreed by solemn definition as though her other decisions might be presumed to be false or putting forward insufficient motive for truth and honesty. Quite to the contrary, a characteristic of all true followers of Christ, lettered or unlettered, is to allow themselves to be guided and led in all things that touch upon faith or morals by the Holy Church of God through its Supreme Pastor the Roman Pontiff, who is himself guided by Jesus Christ Our Lord.

Importance of Instruction

105. Consequently, since everything must be referred to the law and mind of God, in order to bring about the universal and permanent restoration of marriage, it is indeed of the utmost importance that the faithful should be well instructed concerning matrimony; both by word of mouth and by the written word, not cursorily but often and fully, by means of plain and weighty arguments, so that these truths will strike the intellect and will be deeply engraved on their hearts. Let them realize and diligently reflect upon the great wisdom, kindness and bounty God has shown towards the human race, not only by

the institution of marriage, but also, and quite as much, by upholding it with sacred laws; still more, in wonderfully raising it to the dignity of a Sacrament by which such an abundant fountain of graces has been opened to those joined in Christian wedlock, that these may be able to serve the noble purposes of wedlock for their own welfare and for that of their children, of the community and also for that of human relationship.

106. Certainly, if the latter day subverters of marriage are entirely devoted to misleading the minds of men and corrupting their hearts, to making a mockery of matrimonial purity and extolling the filthiest of vices by means of books and pamphlets and other innumerable methods, much more ought you, Venerable Brethren, whom "the Holy Ghost has placed as bishops, to rule the Church of God, which He hath purchased with His own blood,"[82] to give yourselves wholly to this, that through yourselves and through the priests subject to you, and, moreover, through the laity welded together by Catholic Action, so much desired and recommended by Us, into a power of hierarchical apostolate, you may, by every fitting means, oppose error by truth, vice by the excellent dignity of chastity, the slavery of covetousness by the liberty of the sons of God,[83] that disastrous ease in obtaining

---

82   *Acts*, XX, 28.
83   John, VIII, 32 sqq.; Gal., V, 13.

divorce by an enduring love in the bond of marriage and by the inviolate pledge of fidelity given even to death.

107. Thus will it come to pass that the faithful will wholeheartedly thank God that they are bound together by His command and led by gentle compulsion to fly as far as possible from every kind of idolatry of the flesh and from the base slavery of the passions. They will, in a great measure, turn and be turned away from these abominable opinions which to the dishonor of man's dignity are now spread about in speech and in writing and collected under the title of "perfect marriage" and which indeed would make that perfect marriage nothing better than "depraved marriage," as it has been rightly and truly called.

108. Such wholesome instruction and religious training in regard to Christian marriage will be quite different from that exaggerated physiological education by means of which, in these times of ours, some reformers of married life make pretense of helping those joined in wedlock, laying much stress on these physiological matters, in which is learned rather the art of sinning in a subtle way than the virtue of living chastely.

109. So, Venerable Brethren, we make entirely Our own the words which Our predecessor of happy memory, Leo XIII, in his encyclical letter on Christian marriage addressed to the

bishops of the whole world: "Take care not to spare your efforts and authority in bringing about that among the people committed to your guidance that doctrine may be preserved whole and unadulterated which Christ the Lord and the apostles, the interpreters of the divine will, have handed down, and which the Catholic Church herself has religiously preserved, and commanded to be observed by the faithful of every age."[84]

What Spouses Must Do

110. Even the very best instruction given by the Church, however, will not alone suffice to bring about once more conformity of marriage to the law of God; something more is needed in addition to the education of the mind, namely a steadfast determination of the will, on the part of husband and wife, to observe the sacred laws of God and of nature in regard to marriage. In fine, in spite of what others may wish to assert and spread abroad by word of mouth or in writing, let husband and wife resolve: to stand fast to the commandments of God in all things that matrimony demands; always to render to each other the assistance of mutual love; to preserve the honor of chastity; not to lay profane hands on the stable nature of the bond; to use the rights given them by marriage in a

---

84   Encycl. *Arcanum*. 10 Febr. 1880.

way that will be always Christian and sacred, more especially in the first years of wedlock, so that should there be need of continence afterwards, custom will have made it easier for each to preserve it. In order that they may make this firm resolution, keep it and put it into practice, an oft-repeated consideration of their state of life, and a diligent reflection on the sacrament they have received, will be of great assistance to them. Let them constantly keep in mind that they have been sanctified and strengthened for the duties and for the dignity of their state by a special sacrament, the efficacious power of which, although it does not impress a character, is undying. To this purpose we may ponder over the words full of real comfort of holy Cardinal Robert Bellarmine, who with other well-known theologians with devout conviction thus expresses himself: "The sacrament of matrimony can be regarded in two ways: first, in the making, and then in its permanent state. For it is a sacrament like to that of the Eucharist, which not only when it is being conferred, but also whilst it remains, is a sacrament; for as long as the married parties are alive, so long is their union a sacrament of Christ and the Church."[85]

111. Yet in order that the grace of this sacrament may produce its full fruit, there is need,

---

85 St. Rob. Bellarmin., *De controversiis*, tom. III, *De Matr.*, controvers. II, cap. 6.

as we have already pointed out, of the cooperation of the married parties; which consists in their striving to fulfill their duties to the best of their ability and with unwearied effort. For just as in the natural order men must apply the powers given them by God with their own toil and diligence that these may exercise their full vigor, failing which, no profit is gained, so also men must diligently and unceasingly use the powers given them by the grace which is laid up in the soul by this sacrament. Let not, then, those who are joined in matrimony neglect the grace of the sacrament which is in them;[86] for, in applying themselves to the careful observance, however laborious, of their duties they will find the power of that grace becoming more effectual as time goes on. And if ever they should feel themselves to be overburdened by the hardships of their condition of life, let them not lose courage, but rather let them regard in some measure as addressed to them that which St. Paul the Apostle wrote to his beloved disciple Timothy regarding the sacrament of holy Orders when the disciple was dejected through hardship and insults: "I admonish thee that thou stir up the grace which is in thee by the imposition of my hands. For God hath not given us the spirit of fear; but of power, and of love, and of sobriety."[87]

---

86 I *Tim.*, IV,14.
87 II *Tim.*, 1, 6–7.

Due Preparation for Marriage

112. All these things, however, Venerable Brethren, depend in large measure on the due preparation remote and proximate, of the parties for marriage. For it cannot be denied that the basis of a happy wedlock, and the ruin of an unhappy one, is prepared and set in the souls of boys and girls during the period of childhood and adolescence. There is danger that those who before marriage sought in all things what is theirs, who indulged even their impure desires, will be in the married state what they were before, that they will reap that which they have sown;[88] indeed, within the home there will be sadness, lamentation, mutual contempt, strifes, estrangements, weariness of common life, and, worst of all, such parties will find themselves left alone with their own unconquered passions.

113. Let, then, those who are about to enter on married life, approach that state well disposed and well prepared, so that they will be able, as far as they can, to help each other in sustaining the vicissitudes of life, and yet more in attending to their eternal salvation and in forming the inner man unto the fullness of the age of Christ.[89] It will also help them, if they behave towards their cherished offspring as God wills: that is, that the father be

---

88   *Gal.*, VI. 9.
89   *Eph.*, IV, 13.

truly a father, and the mother truly a mother; through their devout love and unwearying care, the home, though it suffer the want and hardship of this valley of tears, may become for the children in its own way a foretaste of that paradise of delight in which the Creator placed the first men of the human race. Thus will they be able to bring up their children as perfect men and perfect Christians; they will instill into them a sound understanding of the Catholic Church, and will give them such a disposition and love for their fatherland as duty and gratitude demand.

114. Consequently, both those who are now thinking of entering upon this sacred married state, as well as those who have the charge of educating Christian youth, should, with due regard to the future, prepare that which is good, obviate that which is bad, and recall those points about which We have already spoken in Our encyclical letter concerning education: "The inclinations of the will, if they are bad, must be repressed from childhood, but such as are good must be fostered, and the mind, particularly of children, should be imbued with doctrines which begin with God, while the heart should be strengthened with the aids of divine grace, in the absence of which, no one can curb evil desires, nor can his discipline and formation be brought to complete perfection by the Church. For Christ has provided her with heavenly doctrines and divine sacraments, that He might make her an effectual teacher of men."[90]

115. To the proximate preparation of a good married life belongs very specially the care in choosing a partner; on that depends a great deal whether the forthcoming marriage will be happy or not, since one may be to the other either a great help in leading a Christian life, or a great danger and hindrance. And so that they may not deplore for the rest of their lives the sorrows arising from an indiscreet marriage, those about to enter into wedlock should carefully deliberate in choosing the person with whom henceforward they must live continually: they should, in so deliberating, keep before their minds the thought first of God and of the true religion of Christ, then of themselves, of their partner, of the children to come, as also of human and civil society, for which wedlock is a fountainhead. Let them diligently pray for divine help, so that they make their choice in accordance with Christian prudence, not indeed led by the blind and unrestrained impulse of lust, nor by any desire of riches or other base influence, but by a true and noble love and by a sincere affection for the future partner; and then let them strive in their married life for those ends for which the [married] state was constituted by God. Lastly, let them not omit to ask the

---

90 Encycl. *Divini illius Magistri*, 31 Dec. 1929.

prudent advice of their parents with regard to the partner, and let them regard this advice in no light manner, in order that by their [i.e., the parents'] mature knowledge and experience of human affairs, they may guard against a disastrous choice, and, on the threshold of matrimony, may receive more abundantly the divine blessing of the fourth commandment: "Honor thy father and thy mother (which is the first commandment with a promise) that it may be well with thee and thou mayest be long-lived upon the earth."[91]

Material Goods and Support of the Family

116. Now since it is no rare thing to find that the perfect observance of God's commands and conjugal integrity encounter difficulties by reason of the fact that the man and wife are in straitened circumstances, their necessities must be relieved as far as possible.

117. And so, in the first place, every effort must be made to bring about that which Our predecessor Leo XIII, of happy memory, has already insisted upon,[92] namely, that in the State such economic and social methods should be adopted as will enable every head of a family to earn as much as, according to his station in life, is necessary for himself,

---

91   *Eph.*, VI, 2–3; *Exod.*, XX, 12.
92   Encycl. *Rerum novarum*, 15 May 1891.

his wife, and for the rearing of his children, for "the laborer is worthy of his hire."[93] To deny this, or to make light of what is equitable, is a grave injustice and is placed among the greatest sins by Holy Scripture;[94] nor is it lawful to fix such a scanty wage as will be insufficient for the upkeep of the family in the circumstances in which it is placed.

118. Care, however, must be taken that the parties themselves, for a considerable time before entering upon married life, should strive to dispose of, or at least to diminish, the material obstacles in their way. The manner in which this may be done effectively and honestly must be pointed out by those who are experienced. Provision must be made also, in the case of those who are not self-supporting, for joint aid by private or public guilds.[95]

119. When these means which We have pointed out do not fulfill the needs, particularly of a larger or poorer family, Christian charity towards our neighbor absolutely demands that those things which are lacking to the needy should be provided; hence it is incumbent on the rich to help the poor, so that, having an abundance of this world's goods, they may not expend them fruitlessly or completely squander them, but employ them for the support

---

93   Luke, X, 7.
94   *Deut.* XXIV, 14, 15.
95   Leo XIII, Encycl. *Rerum novarum*, 15 May 1891.

and well-being of those who lack the necessities of life. They who give of their substance to Christ in the person of His poor will receive from the Lord a most bountiful reward when He shall come to judge the world; they who act to the contrary will pay the penalty.[96] Not in vain does the Apostle warn us: "He that hath the substance of this world and shall see his brother in need, and shall shut up his bowels from him: how doth the charity of God abide in him?"[97]

120. If, however, for this purpose, private resources do not suffice, it is the duty of the public authority to supply for the insufficient forces of individual effort, particularly in a matter which is of such importance to the common weal, touching as it does the maintenance of the family and married people. If families, particularly those in which there are many children, have not suitable dwellings; if the husband cannot find employment and means of livelihood; if the necessities of life cannot be purchased except at exorbitant prices; if even the mother of the family, to the great harm of the home, is compelled to go forth and seek a living by her own labor; if she, too, in the ordinary or even extraordinary labors of childbirth, is deprived of proper food, medicine, and the assistance of a skilled

96   Matth., XXV, 34 sqq.
97   *I John*, III, 17.

physician, it is patent to all to what an extent married people may lose heart, and how home life and the observance of God's commands are rendered difficult for them; indeed it is obvious how great a peril can arise to the public security and to the welfare and very life of civil society itself when such men are reduced to that condition of desperation that, having nothing which they fear to lose, they are emboldened to hope for chance advantage from the upheaval of the state and of established order.

121. Wherefore, those who have the care of the State and of the public good cannot neglect the needs of married people and their families, without bringing great harm upon the State and on the common welfare. Hence, in making the laws and in disposing of public funds they must do their utmost to relieve the needs of the poor, considering such a task as one of the most important of their administrative duties.

122. We are sorry to note that not infrequently nowadays it happens that through a certain inversion of the true order of things, ready and bountiful assistance is provided for the unmarried mother and her illegitimate offspring (who, of course, must be helped in order to avoid a greater evil) which is denied to legitimate mothers or given sparingly or almost grudgingly.

Good Laws Concerning Marriage and Family

123. But not only in regard to temporal goods, Venerable Brethren, is it the concern of the public authority to make proper provision for matrimony and the family, but also in other things which concern the good of souls. Just laws must be made for the protection of chastity, for reciprocal conjugal aid, and for similar purposes, and these must be faithfully enforced, because, as history testifies, the prosperity of the State and the temporal happiness of its citizens cannot remain safe and sound where the foundation on which they are established, which is the moral order, is weakened and where the very fountainhead from which the State draws its life, namely, wedlock and the family, is obstructed by the vices of its citizens.

124. For the preservation of the moral order neither the laws and sanctions of the temporal power are sufficient, nor is the beauty of virtue and the expounding of its necessity. Religious authority must enter in to enlighten the mind, to direct the will, and to strengthen human frailty by the assistance of divine grace. Such an authority is found nowhere save in the Church instituted by Christ the Lord. Hence We earnestly exhort in the Lord all those who hold the reins of power that they establish and maintain firmly harmony and friendship with this Church of Christ so that through the united activity and energy of both powers the tremendous evils, fruits of those wanton liberties which assail both marriage and the family and are a menace to both Church and State, may be effectively frustrated.

125. Governments can assist the Church greatly in the execution of its important office, if, in laying down their ordinances, they take account of what is prescribed by divine and ecclesiastical law, and if penalties are fixed for offenders. For as it is, there are those who think that whatever is permitted by the laws of the State, or at least is not punished by them, is allowed also in the moral order, and, because they neither fear God nor see any reason to fear the laws of man, they act even against their conscience, thus often bringing ruin upon themselves and upon many others. There will be no peril to or lessening of the rights and integrity of the State from its association with the Church. Such suspicion and fear is empty and groundless, as Leo XIII has already so clearly set forth: "It is generally agreed," he says, "that the Founder of the Church, Jesus Christ, wished the spiritual power to be distinct from the civil, and each to be free and unhampered in doing its own work, not forgetting, however, that it is expedient to both, and in the interest of everybody, that there be a harmonious relationship... If the civil power combines in a friendly manner with the spiritual power of the Church, it necessarily follows

that both parties will greatly benefit. The dignity of the State will be enhanced, and with religion as its guide, there will never be a rule that is not just; while for the Church there will be at hand a safeguard and defense which will operate to the public good of the faithful."[98]

126. To bring forward a recent and clear example of what is meant, it has happened quite in consonance with right order and entirely according to the law of Christ, that in the solemn Convention happily entered into between the Holy See and the Kingdom of Italy, also in matrimonial affairs a peaceful settlement and friendly cooperation has been obtained, such as befitted the glorious history of the Italian people and its ancient and sacred traditions. These decrees are to be found in the Lateran Pact: "The Italian State, desirous of restoring to the institution of matrimony, which is the basis of the family, that dignity conformable to the traditions of its people, assigns as civil effects of the sacrament of matrimony all that is attributed to it in Canon Law."[99] To this fundamental norm are added further clauses in the common pact.

127. This might well be a striking example to all of how, even in this our own day (in which, sad to say, the absolute separation of

98   Encycl. *Arcanum divinae sapientiae*, 10 Febr. 1880.
99   Concord., art. 34; Act. *Apost. Sed.*, XXI (1929), pag. 290.

the civil power from the Church, and indeed from every religion, is so often taught), the one supreme authority can be united and associated with the other without detriment to the rights and supreme power of either, thus protecting Christian parents from pernicious evils and menacing ruin.

128. All these things which, Venerable Brethren, prompted by Our past solicitude We put before you, We wish according to the norm of Christian prudence to be promulgated widely among all Our beloved children committed to your care as members of the great family of Christ, that all may be thoroughly acquainted with sound teaching concerning marriage, so that they may be ever on their guard against the dangers advocated by the teachers of error, and most of all, that "denying ungodliness and worldly desires, they may live soberly and justly and godly in this world, looking for the blessed hope and coming of the glory of the great God and our Savior Jesus Christ."[100]

129. May the Father, "of whom all paternity in heaven and earth is named,"[101] Who strengthens the weak and gives courage to the pusillanimous and fainthearted; and Christ our Lord and Redeemer, "the Institutor and Perfecter of the holy sacraments,"[102] Who

---

100   *Tit.*, II, 12–13.
101   *Eph.*, I III, 15.
102   Conc. Trid., Sess. XXIV.

desired marriage to be and made it the mystical image of His own ineffable union with the Church; and the Holy Ghost, Love of God, the Light of hearts and the Strength of the mind, grant that all will perceive, will admit with a ready will, and by the grace of God will put into practice, what We by this letter have expounded concerning the holy sacrament of matrimony, the wonderful law and will of God respecting it, the errors and impending dangers, and the remedies with which they can be counteracted, so that that fruitfulness dedicated to God will flourish again vigorously in Christian wedlock.

130. We most humbly pour forth Our earnest prayer at the Throne of His Grace, that God, the Author of all graces, the inspirer of all good desires and deeds,[103] may bring this about, and deign to give it bountifully according to the greatness of His liberality and omnipotence, and as a token of the abundant blessing of the same Omnipotent God, We most lovingly grant to you, Venerable Brethren, and to the clergy and people committed to your watchful care, the Apostolic Benediction.

Given at Rome, in Saint Peter's,
this 31st day of December, of the year 1930,
the ninth of Our Pontificate.

✠ Pius XI

---

103 *Phil.*, II, 13.

A GUIDED
READING

1

What is chaste marriage?
(1–9)

In the first part of the encyclical,[1] Pope Pius XI tells us that marriage is "of its very nature" a divine institution.

For us who are raised on the milk of self-actualization, this one concept might take a while to absorb. We are in the habit of thinking that we make up institutions as we go along. To change the paradigm, I recommend a close and careful reading of the first two chapters of Genesis – in particular, Genesis 1:27 and Genesis 2:24. These two passages help us see what the encyclical teaches: that God gave mankind the covenant of marriage. He made them male and female, two. In his covenant, the two become one flesh. That is marriage "from the beginning."

We begin to appreciate that God has something specific in mind about marriage, and,

_____

1   In this guide, my commentary will refer to passages from the document using paragraph numbers in parentheses.

reading along with Pius, we get the inkling that if we can accept and conform our ideas to His, we will achieve peace.

That's the kind of thing that a lot of people today have trouble doing — conforming their ideas to someone else's — even supposing they can agree that this "someone else" has authority.

Now, skepticism of authority is often a salutary impulse, as many authorities aren't trustworthy, or at least need constant supervision to keep corruption at bay.

But if you think about it, God, by *definition*, must be Good — thus, what He says must also be True. *If* that's so, we can accept His authority. Maybe we need some convincing on this, however, so let's get back to the text of the encyclical.

Early on in the document (paragraph 3), Pius XI speaks of looking with a paternal eye on the universal world as from a watchtower. It's lovely to stop worrying for a moment and feel the force of this metaphor.

The watchtower is the view from above — the place of vigil where the signs of danger are acted upon for the good of the innocents below. It's a watchtower over a forest or a city, not a prison — a place where the vision can be clear and help can be quick.

Pius XI's use of this image perhaps brings to mind a sermon from St. Gregory the Great, the last pope to be revered by the Orthodox, Anglicans and other Protestants, and Catholics alike. In it Gregory references Ezekiel 33 in which God calls the prophet to be a watchman for the house of Israel.

Gregory remarks, "A watchman always stands on a height so that he can see from afar what is coming. Anyone appointed to be a watchman for the people must stand on a height for all his life to help them by his foresight." He goes on to say, "Truly the all-powerful Creator and Redeemer of mankind can give me in spite of my weaknesses a higher life and effective speech; because I love him, I do not spare myself in speaking of him."

And this is what he sees, this pope—Pius XI, of the early 20th century, a century that we know turned out very badly for so many hundreds of millions of the innocent: He sees that things are in a bad way. But we must remember that God has a plan; man can carry out that plan in each instance. A man and a woman freely enter into the married state—*but they have no freedom as to what that state is.*

They can do well or ill.

But they can't change what the *plan* is.

Marriage is a sacrament and, by the means of Christ's redemption, has been restored to the original purity of its divine institution (that is, the purity intended by God when He instituted it at the beginning of Creation).

Here is the foundation for the unchangeable nature of matrimony. It's no use thinking of marriage as something like a set of blocks out of which you can build whatever you want. Instead, the Church wants us to see that it is truly the very oldest institution *and a covenant* – founded, as the encyclical points out, in the very first chapter of Genesis.

Marriage is less like a construct, an arbitrary convenience, and more like water that you can drink or not drink – but as to its use in your body, and its necessity, you have no say. It is what it is.

In order to understand what follows – and to catch the message – we have to accept the premise that marriage is just this: Given to us by a loving God.

Here is where that suspension of disbelief I spoke of in the preface might be needed. We've been trained from our earliest years, some of us, to think of marriage quite differently.

If we are going to read and understand, we must accept the premises – just for now! Perhaps rather than trying to spend time establishing God's *bona fides* when it comes to telling us what to do, we might read and be convinced of what He has said when we honestly consult our experience and common sense; and that conviction will help us to believe that He *is* both good and true, and that He is to be trusted.

2

God has no grandchildren
(11–18)

The Goods of Marriage are three. Children, Fidelity, and Sacrament.

The hardest of these – to talk about and be understood – is children.

And the reason it's hard is because we have fallen into a modern tendency to think in terms of Individual vs. The Rest of the World.

When we read paragraph 10 of this document, some might get the wrong idea and become a little panicky at the thought that marriage might be something else other than a big "me" project.

We have to step back, just for a moment, even if it makes us just a little anxious at first, from all our ideas about ourselves as individuals.

We must remind ourselves, going back to the intimate details of the Creation account in Genesis, that God made man and woman in His image, and that the Image of God is fruitfulness. Father, Son, Holy Spirit – the Persons love each other, are Love, and that love spills over with unimaginable fruitfulness into creation. This is *how* God made man to love.

Thus, when we form a family, by nature (and I use the word in all senses), its purpose is fruitfulness.

Fruitful is what it *is*. Children are the fruit.

Now, we see this in nature. Biology dictates that living things are, above all, oriented to reproduction. But man is different in that he doesn't procreate mindlessly, but with love, and in the context of the family. **(11)**

Children are necessary for mankind to exist. Have we come to the point where we don't think this? Yes! We have! In an astonishing departure from reality, we have managed to forget the necessity of children.

We tend to think that all the inventions, institutions, efforts, and energy – all the neighborhoods, communities, towns, cities, countries – on this earth are for individuals, or sometimes we might think they are for "society," which in turn for us is a collection of individuals.

But actually, it's all for children – children in families.

It's all for the protection of children. It's all

so that we have the peace we need to be able to teach our children what they need to know to grow up and have their own children.

They are not individuals so much as persons. And so are we.

Ultimately, this procreation has a divine purpose as well as a natural one. Life is more than what we find here on earth. We are really meant to give everything back to God, and to be with Him when we die. (12)

That's the covenant He made with our first parents.

Things get a little tricky in paragraph 13.

I call this the "God has no grandchildren" doctrine of spiritual generation.

You see, Original Sin—the sin in which Adam and Eve sinned decisively, once for all, which we call The Fall—is passed on by *generation*—it's in our DNA, so to speak. If you think about it just a little, you will see how this must be so.

The fallenness has to be acquired somehow. If you think of it as a condition, the way C. S. Lewis did, it makes it easier to understand. This condition is passed on by the very fact of being born human. Our *nature* didn't change when Adam and Eve fell, but it became subject to living under a cloud.

Any other way of contracting this fallenness would take away its universality. We might start to think that somehow man might be perfectible, if only we could raise him up properly from the beginning. Some people do think this, in the face of all evidence, which is that there is something about being conceived human that brings the fallenness with it.

That is the idea of "generation"—the generative act itself—being the source of Original Sin.

Later we will see that this necessarily entails the corollary that sex is the means of perpetuating Original Sin. Of course, since humans are generated through the sexual act—we don't reproduce by splitting or grafting!—it's easy to then conclude that sex is sinful.

Easy, but wrong.

So it's best to get this whole question straightened out now. The sexual act between the spouses is covenanted—it's good and holy. (Remember that the encyclical begins with the reminder that Jesus' Atonement restores marriage to its original, pre-Fall purity.)

The *means*, however, of transmitting Original Sin is through that act. That is all.

The remedy to Original Sin is, of course, Baptism. And this is the spiritual regeneration that the family offers to the children, to bring them into the kingdom.

Because God has no grandchildren.

He has children.

Each child must become His child.

The best way — the way He ordained — is for each child to become His child by means of the loving education provided by his parents, not by generation, that is, natural life. By *re*-generation — that is, Baptism.

So just as the earthly realm is augmented by the fruit of generation, the spiritual one is augmented by the fruit of regeneration.

This is what makes being a mother so joyful (14). To cooperate with God in His outpouring of creativity is an amazing privilege. It's she who lovingly teaches her husband to be a father by means of her motherhood, as Saint John Paul II has told us in his exhortation *Mulieris Dignitatem* (On the Dignity and Vocation of Woman). The whole enterprise of begetting and educating children is an awe-inspiring, two-fold adventure, both natural and supernatural. (15–18)

This is it! In this adventure the whole of earthly and heavenly experience is contained! Fruitfulness, loving nurturing, careful tending. Mother, father, child.

If we don't understand this we won't understand anything about this document. Step back. See that the workings of the world, if they are to be just and good, turn on how we value the primary place of the child.

We'll look at the other two goods of marriage in the next sections.

3

"You are building something"
(19–30)

Once, long ago, Mr. Lawler and I were taping a TV interview for a Catholic program. Another guest was a young man who had overcome addiction to drugs and all sorts of adversity to come home to the Lord. I can't remember anything about the whole episode except a little exchange we had in the parking lot afterwards.

This young man was full of that energy and intensity that, if not channeled, often do land a person in difficulties. I liked him. He asked if the hosts (an older married couple) and Phil and I would like to go out to grab a bite after our interviews were over, and honestly, I would have enjoyed that.

But we were young parents with at least four (can't quite remember) very young children at home – children who were almost certainly being naughty right at that moment and driving their grandmother crazy; and we were at least 45 minutes away from home. If nothing else, staying out late would make the next day somewhat purgatorial.

We looked at each other, my husband gave the eyebrow (you know, the "thumbs-down" eyebrow), and we cheerfully made our excuses. We were genuinely sorry not to be able to get to know him better, but we explained our situation and took our leave.

As we parted, this young fellow said, "It's okay! I have nothing to go home to. You–you are building something."

That is the meaning of fidelity in marriage.

When you are married, you are building something. Whether you know it or not, that is what you are doing. Only time will reveal what that something is.

Some things take a short time to build. A family takes a lifetime.

Just as in the previous section, we need to step back from our worries and anxieties and see what this thing is that we are working on, this lifetime project.

Read the text to hear this message that is so lost today.

Read it.

If you look at it through the lens of power, you will understand nothing. If you look at it through the lens of love — the kind of love we all want, which is the love that wants the good of the other — you will find wisdom!

An example of this wisdom is when Pius says (23) that the couple must have "an especially holy and pure love, not as adulterers love each other." He is asking us to put our sexual love in the context of the whole of God's plan. To keep it free of anything ugly, pornographic, or vulgar. Let's be honest here. Pornography is a multi-billion dollar industry and shows every sign of gaining mainstream acceptance and normalization, if fashion and entertainment are any indication.

Maybe that goes without saying, but maybe not.

Now, there's this:

> This outward expression of love in the home demands not only mutual help but must go further; must have as its primary purpose that man and wife help each other day by day in forming and perfecting themselves in the interior life, so that through their partnership in life they may advance ever more and more in virtue, and above all that they may grow in true love toward God and their neighbor, on which indeed "dependeth the whole Law and the Prophets." (23)

What is this interior life that he speaks of? Ah, a world ... the Kingdom of Heaven is within. And marriage is not only being a family and educating children, but more:

> The blending of life as a whole and the mutual interchange and sharing thereof. (24)

Life! And then there's this:

> Domestic society being confirmed, therefore, by this bond of love, there should flourish in it that "order of love," as St. Augustine calls it. This order includes both the primacy of the husband with regard to the wife and children, the ready subjection of the wife and her willing obedience, which the Apostle commends in these words: "Let women be subject to their husbands as to the Lord, because the husband is the head of the wife, and Christ is the head of the Church." (26)

These words are hard for us, but before turning away, look at the words "confirmed ... by this bond of love." And go back and read (23) again.

> This precept the Apostle laid down when he said: "Husbands, love your wives as Christ also loved the Church," that Church which of a

> truth He embraced with a bound-
> less love not for the sake of His
> own advantage, but seeking only
> the good of His Spouse.

The helpful discussion, the one where we rise above our limited view conditioned by the concept of equality, begins after having a look at (27): "does not deny liberty . . . nor does it bid her obey every request not in harmony with right reason or dignity."

Let me try to unpack this for you according to the text (although we will grapple with the submission-of-the-wife issue more fully in a later discussion, and I beg you to be sure you make it that far!).

The Church is trying her hardest to protect you from two evils.

First, it's just missing the point to think that in marriage, the husband gets a slave or even wants a slave. He married his wife because he loves her and wants to build a life with her. He is a work in progress himself, and he knows it. She is like him in a way no other creature is or can be: "Flesh of my flesh, bone of my bone" (Gen 2:23).

Many women in our post-feminist culture show no respect for their husbands – even the respect due to another human being, let alone one you have committed yourself to for life.

But other women adopt a false subservience. Sometimes these women have a subservience that veils a contemptuous and discontented attitude that ultimately destroys the friendship that ought to come about in marriage, understood in the Aristotelian sense of equals whose lives are united. Neither of these types of woman will readily yield in anything, large or small. (This topic warrants its own discussion, but for now, let's move on.)

Sometimes a woman understands submission to mean that she ought to give up her personhood, under the mistaken impression that one ceases to be the author of one's own acts by becoming a wife. Of course the husband ought not to be a petty demi-god who demands offerings. According to the Catholic Church, he *must not* be. The wife is not a child. It is a sin against the love this document is talking about, which is ultimate, sanctifying love, for him to be anything but sacrificial in his love and honor for his wife.

The second evil the Church is guarding against has to do with the fact that no one knows what challenges life will bring. Jobs. Unemployment. Moving. Sickness. Danger. Your adventure of love, your marriage, requires *unity*.

Why must the primacy (headship) belong to the man? Now we are approaching the mystery. Part of it is that men and women are equal (having been formed by God from the same substance), *but* different and complementary.

Reality is hierarchical—did you know that? The concept of hierarchy is quite unexplored in modern society, yet it is real. What is marvelous is that supernatural hierarchy reflects something that is in God, which was summed up by St. Paul when he said that Jesus, one of the Persons of the Trinity, did not deem equality something to be grasped at (Philippians 2:6).

You are making a mistake—an utterly modern mistake—if you equate hierarchy with inequality, or think that it demeans a wife, the heart of her family, to grant primacy to her head, her husband.

Husbands: Your wife is making a sanctuary for you, as well as all the other things she does. *Your* home. This sanctuary is hidden from most. But it is your delight. Belittle this gift at your peril.

Wives: Your husband is making it possible for you to be the maker of a sanctuary, the heart of what you build together. If you tear it down with your own hands, you are tearing out your own heart. (Proverbs 14)

And let's not skip too lightly over paragraph 28, in which the document readily affirms that subjection varies according to conditions.

In other words, you, husband and wife, are free to interpret this according to many criteria, including your personalities and temperaments. Once, that is, you have absorbed the irreducible principles.

Just keep in mind that "the structure of the family and its fundamental law (unity and fidelity: 'The two shall be one flesh'), established and confirmed by God, must always and everywhere be maintained intact."

4

What kind of wall serves our city best?
(31–42)

If your idea about marriage reflects what most people think and is shaped by how they act, then marriage would appear to be a most private, tenuous, and contingent kind of relationship, hardly even rising to the dignity of an institution.

In a world where new buildings, as an architect of a large complex at a premier university said, apparently without irony, "can last fifty years," it's not surprising that our culture does not expect a marriage to endure.

The Church has a different idea. Marriage is established by God as His first covenant with the first man and woman. Its whole purpose is to be an un-mechanistic mechanism whereby, through love, human society can flourish, each generation in its stability and unity passing along to the next what it means to be part of this adventure.

Marriage is meant to be the sanctuary where each child can become a child of God and know Him as a father. In justice, it's meant to be a rock for each person. The faithfulness of the husband and wife build something that lasts beyond them.

What's amazing is that all this is just part of being human. It's not reserved for the few, the chosen, but rather, this truth is written into the soul of each man and woman – what St. John Paul II called "the nuptial [marital] meaning of the body."

Being a man, being a woman, was intended by God to mean "made for each other in His plan."

> Wherefore, both for the private good of husband, wife and children, as likewise for the public good of human society, they indeed deserve well who strenuously defend the inviolable stability of matrimony. (37)

"Defend" – even in the face of all the exceptions that can be piled up to the moon. An exception really does prove the rule, and who is to blame if the rule gets buried under the pile?

Chesterton said:

> A wall is like a rule; and the gates are like the exceptions that prove the rule. The man making it has to

decide where his rule will run and where his exceptions shall stand. He cannot have a city that is all gates any more than a house that is all windows; nor is it possible to have a law that consists entirely of liberties.

I think it's not too much to ask that we as a culture just take a little time to think about what kind of *wall* serves our city best. A respite from the incessant talk of liberties might help us to ponder the limits and standards we actually need.

Even better, what kind of wall did *God* give us to build the city with? It is in paragraph 36 that the whole of this teaching turns:

> The marriage of Christians recalls that most perfect union which exists between Christ and the Church: *Sacramentum hoc magnum est, ego autem dico, in Christo et in ecclesia* [This is a great mystery, but I speak concerning Christ and the Church]. (Ephesians 5:32)

We are free persons. We are free to do our best to try to mirror Christ's love for the Church ... or we can surrender to a different understanding.

But if we surrender (and actually, this is not a hypothetical, but amply demonstrated), then we can't be surprised when people *also give up* on the Church, Christ's love, and indeed, the Fatherhood of God.

That's what that passage means. The two are linked.

Later we will grapple with the exceptions and what-ifs and necessary worries and contingencies.

But right now, we just have to have some criteria — some standards — and those standards should be rooted in who we are and how God made us. Our standards should not be arbitrary or based on our particular preferences. And we should recognize that they are, above all, not constructs. They are given, not fashioned according to our will. That's what the document has been about up until now.

Then it goes further.

Marriage is a sacrament, and that's what these next paragraphs (38–42) are about.

For those readers who might not know what a sacrament is, or who might have only a hazy, somewhat metaphorical idea, here is a quick primer.

The sacraments, and there are seven instituted by Christ Himself when He walked on earth, are, in the words of the Catechism,

> ... efficacious signs of grace, insti-
> tuted by Christ and entrusted to
> the Church, by which divine life is
> dispensed to us. The visible rites by
> which the sacraments are celebrated
> signify and make present the graces
> proper to each sacrament. They
> bear fruit in those who receive them
> with the required dispositions. (*Cat-
> echism of the Catholic Church*, 1131)

In other words, a sacrament *is* what it *signifies*. It isn't *just* a sign, like a 35-mph sign that signifies that you may go that speed, but doesn't give you the power or grace to do so. But the sacrament of Baptism, for instance, gives you life in Christ and washes you with his blood and gives you the grace to be his child. It's a ritual, but not an empty one. This ritual has meaning *and* effect. In the case of the sacrament of marriage, it has *mutual* effect for the spouses, uniting them each other and to Christ until death.

Marriage as a human institution is endowed with dignity and nobility, as we've seen. Marriage as a covenant between baptized persons, freely entered into, is a sign that *is* what it *signifies*.

It signifies unity and the building of something larger than ourselves. It signifies love that overflows into the creation and nurturing of new life. It signifies faithfulness and cleaving together. (38, 39)

And it is all those things in a supernatural way. It reaches back, past the fallenness that taints everything we do, to that first pure covenant—by the grace of God. It is a liturgical event, flowing from the Sacrifice of the Altar, the Eucharist, and united to it.

In his novel *That Hideous Strength*, C. S. Lewis remarked, "I suppose the mere fact of being walled in gave the Wood part of its peculiar quality, for when a thing is enclosed, the mind does not willingly regard it as common." The wall is a sign of the sacred; this wall of marriage is what it signifies.

Marriage gives grace, bears fruit—in those who are open (**40, 41**).

So if you are feeling that somehow these noble thoughts don't reflect *your* marriage, take a moment to re-read those last few paragraphs (**40–42**). And if you're not married yet, think about how this might be a bit different from how you've viewed the whole enterprise up until now.

5

Her truly regal throne
(44–93)

It should be the work of a quick discussion to handle the topics of marriage as social construct, divorce, contraception, abortion, "other errors," and whether working makes a woman a wage slave.

Shouldn't take long.

I jest.

But seriously, we need to consult reality to understand this section.

Do you have your reality check in place? You can get it by taking a few minutes to look at the news and listen to your neighbors' problems:

In America, a couple tries to force/bribe the surrogate mother they've hired to abort their child, who turns out not to be *their* child, exactly, but a child of his and an anonymous egg-donor's. Girls in Syria are sent to be child brides and murdered if they protest.

In America, a child has three "parents" registered on her birth certificate. ISIS executes girls who won't have sex with their captors.

In China, the government insists on butchering what they consider superfluous babies. In America, a man was able to butcher near-term babies for years, mutilate and kill women, and lie about the money he made. He was only stopped because of the money, not because of the butchering. It's hard to keep this list up to date; as of this writing, we come to find that what amounts to an arm of the government is in the business of selling organs from babies – organs it harvests while the babies are still alive.

Whole villages in India are run as farms for babies grown by surrogate mothers. An earthquake in Nepal finds the babies being saved by their rich foreign "owners," but the mothers – slaves – are left behind.

And normal, regular families, not exactly facing horrors of this magnitude (yet), still are pressured and poked and prodded by some force outside of them that they can't identify and don't know how to resist.

This is our reality. This is now. This is the world that all the mockers and ignorers of "chaste marriage" made.

I am not under the impression that "before" things were better, and "now" they are worse.

Things have been very bad in the past. We in this country have been blessed with a time of great prosperity and peace for most, although for those in the shameful institution of slavery, the blessing of family was denied them in many cases as a matter of policy. Knowing this injustice and seeing the landscape today in our "more enlightened" times, we can be surprised to discover that even those who, in the first half of the 20th century, faced poverty and terrible discrimination because of their race – at least most of them had families. More than today.

Things are very bad now. At times, when a man and a women freely entered into a lifelong union, supported by law, things have been better, society has flourished, and children have been safe – although children, being weak, are always less safe than they should be.

Still, isn't it interesting that in 1930, the year of the publication of this encyclical, the Catholic Church, not normally one for quick reactions, decided to tackle purveyors of the "marriage as pure product of convention" school of thought?

That's what strikes the reader – how serious these questions seem to us today, and how serious they clearly were, more than eighty years ago.

And so the pope wrote all this, this cry of the pastor, the warning of the watchman. You will recall from the timeline at the beginning of this book the events that became the spur for him to write: The acceptance of contraception (in certain limited cases, presciently foreseen by Pius as quickly burgeoning) by the Anglicans, and the rising influence of Margaret Sanger and her poisonous ideology.

That Marxism and Fascism, both ideologies that seek to control human actions *and thoughts* on every level, were poised to devour whole nations, also motivated him to plead with men and women to do what is right and according to God's plan.

Deep in the heart of this document, he says this about the theory of personal revolution (the personal always being at the core of the universal):

> This [detaching the woman from her spouse and children, recounted in the previous paragraphs], however, is not the true emancipation of woman, nor that rational and exalted liberty which belongs to the noble office of a Christian woman and wife; it is rather the debasing of the womanly character and the dignity of motherhood, and indeed of the whole family, as a result of which the husband suffers the loss of his wife, the children of their mother, and the home and the

whole family of an ever watchful guardian. More than this, this false liberty and unnatural equality with the husband is to the detriment of the woman herself, for if the woman descends from her truly regal throne to which she has been raised within the walls of the home by means of the Gospel, she will soon be reduced to the old state of slavery (if not in appearance, certainly in reality) and become as amongst the pagans the mere instrument of man. (75)

We have lived out his prophecy. Now we see the insidious effect on, well, everything, when the elites (the smart, rich, revolutionizing few) convince the others – the ordinary (less educated, many), their victims, to restructure things away from the home.

It suits the very few to live a certain way, and they have no trouble destroying things for others. The home has always been a refuge for the oppressed and the poor. A man's home truly is his castle – it is a sovereign place, unassailable as a stronghold, even by the rich.

But that is taken from them now.

Especially women, who, despite what they tell you, have always found a way to work if they wanted to, or to work with their families at a common task (like a farm or small business) – but who valued home higher and never relieved themselves of the high calling to make a home – women have been all too willing to accept the reasoning that what the world (men?) call success is truly success.

This conviction has devolved to the absurdity of a woman being extolled on the cover of *Newsweek* as having her highest goal – for herself and for all women – be to succeed. Simply that – succeed to show that women can succeed.

Raw ambition elevated to a higher place than the desire to serve others or to fulfill a talent.

And not just mindless success, but success that purposely admits and even extols trampling on the needs of her children and turning over the building of her home to hired help (of course, in the case of a rich woman, the best help; whether everyone can afford *the best help* or whether money can buy *the best help* at all is left to your imagination and experience).

Success that never even asks about justice to the hired help – undoubtedly also women! – who in a less self-avowedly craven and grasping society, might have a chance at their own – their very own – humble abode, rather than being confined to raising other people's children.

Success in the world (for the very few, remember!) that has the effect of reviling "domesticity" (even the word has a scornful tinge to it, but just means home-keeping).

131

Who among us hasn't heard the word "drudgery" to describe what pertains to the home and its keeping?

The argument here in the encyclical has to be seen for what it is and is not.

It is a simple statement of reality.

The home needs an inviolable heart. It is not a commentary on the validity of a woman's involvement in things outside the home, but a statement of priorities. It is not a proscription against individual expression, but a warning of the quick ascendancy of the will to power when the important, hidden, humble things are lost.

Note that Pius XI identifies *achieving equality* between the sexes as a step *down* for the woman.

So, I think you can read the paragraphs in this section (44–93) yourself and get the gist of them.

Understand them by keeping in mind the degree to which, in the name of justice, *injustice* has been done by convincing women and men that the home *is nothing to sacrifice for.*

In the eyes of the world, it's probably the most quixotic and futile vision possible – the vision in this encyclical. The message of *Casti Connubii* is misinterpreted by modern man and woman as an oppressive one. (Indeed, feminism can count as one of its successes that it shuts down conversation of its goals before that conversation begins.)

Just as the message of Jesus Himself seems impossibly narrow (and He Himself acknowledges that the gate is narrow), so this expression of what the family means, and specifically what the woman means to the family, seems impossible.

* * *

I can't help but think that absolutely no attention will be paid to what it means for a woman to be placed on a "truly regal throne to which she has been raised within the walls of the home by means of the Gospel."

Unless you have the imagination to picture what life is like for women who have the misfortune to be born into a society that does not know God's precepts, you will be misled by the flowery, somewhat 19th-century prose.

Unless you are honest about how women are treated today, you will not appreciate what it means for the humblest woman to be truly exalted in the bosom of her family.

I do get a little impatient with those who force their "facts" about the way women were treated in the "past"—meaning sometime in the dark ages before, say, 1978—in the face of all the evidence, even pictorial, which

133

shows that women were treated with dignity and respect (not least because they respected themselves as having a real effect on society through their faithfulness).

These critics take as historical fact the films and shows produced today—produced, of course, by entertainers thoroughly imbued with feminist dogma. Theirs is a Mad-Men-as-documentary kind of history. They pay no attention to the actual record.

However, if you dare to bring up statistics and the lived experience of this moment as to the utter trashing of anything feminine—the pile of aborted children, the rising tide of unwed mothers, the final objectification of the woman's body—they tune out.

This little encyclical will almost certainly be dismissed as old-fashioned (even though its vision is held up against something older, namely a pagan, view of women). Yet the modern way hasn't worked out very well. I can't see that smiling upon a woman as she leaves her infant in daycare to go earn her share of the national debt represents anything other than enshrining her as a wage-slave, just as the pope said it would.

I don't know what more evidence we need. Is the answer to nail more two-by-fours onto the wreckage? ("However, they should take care lest the calamitous state of their external affairs should be the occasion for a much more calamitous error" [61].)

Or is it to pull away the debris and recover the proper way of building?

The reality of this disturbance of what is truly human as God planned it from the beginning was proclaimed over and over by John Paul II. He tried to convey the divine vision when he said, "All of humanity passes through the family."

Who finally takes responsibility for that ineluctable fact, the one fact that the "progression" of history cannot change – the fact of the family?

Instead of quite despairing, however, or even dwelling further on these "errors" as Pius so quaintly calls them, I leave you here with what I hope is a bracing thought to stiffen the sinews of your resolve.

Back in paragraph 61, Pope Pius XI reminds us of the teaching of the Council of Trent, that it is anathema – *to be condemned* – to hold "that there are precepts of God impossible for the just to observe. God does not ask the impossible, but by His commands, instructs you to do what you are able, to pray for what you are not able that He may help you."

Have faith. Be a person of faith. Once a person determines that a thing would be wrong – and that no force on earth will compel him to do what is wrong—he then finds a way. Even more than finding a way, he finds the joy—she finds the joy—of serving the truth.

6
Two tough bits
(44–93 again)

When I started writing for our blog, *Like Mother, Like Daughter*, my dearest hope grew to be to gently encourage and sometimes forthrightly admonish. If I think that a picture of my kitchen sink or garden will do the former, I will post it. If I think that you need to be told in so many words how to get up earlier (because I remember myself in your shoes), I will do the latter.

My reason was that I know what it's like to have a deep awareness of and longing for something that you don't quite (or at all, even a little bit) know how to achieve. Very often when we don't know how to do something, we think we don't want to do it; and often the converse is true: When we finally figure out how to do something, we find we wanted to do it all along and it makes us happy.

Due to an unfortunate loss of the collective memory, many of us have been in the position of recreating something, the form of which we can hardly conceive. And some of us are seriously impaired and could use a lift from someone who's gone down the road before.

In part, the struggle to live according to a different vision is utterly practical. And in part—the part where we have to fight through early indoctrination and latent, subconscious habit—it is theoretical.

It's the theoretical that I decided to tackle with this reading of *Casti Connubii* (called Chaste Marriage in plain, 19th century English—because Pius XI, writing in 1930, was a 19th century kind of guy). I would put it to you that it's well worth it to figure out how the unbroken tradition of the Church interprets Scripture in the light of current problems; that is to say, expresses that tradition in an encyclical such as this one.

Not to shy away from the tough bits, I would like to expand on a few points that are going to be stumbling blocks for your average 21st-century woman, no matter how committed she thinks she is to living differently.

First tough bit—some teach that marriage can be made into whatever people like, and that the "generative power"—the ability to have children—does not need to be kept within wedlock...

> ... as though to suggest that the
> license of a base fornicating woman
> should enjoy the same rights as the
> chaste motherhood of a lawfully
> wedded wife. (50)

I will not take refuge in any defense that the
writer is *merely* a "product of his time," trying to explain this statement away or ignore
it, although by necessity an encyclical relates
to its time period and the issues thereof. I'd
rather meet it head on.

One reader, when we did *Casti Connubii*
on the blog, said that this seems to be the
harshest statement in the document. I'm sure
it strikes you that way.

Pius XI is talking about the modern (and,
in 1930, already in full swing) project of
redefining marriage and taking the procre-
ative act out of the context of marriage. The
whole encyclical is directed towards defin-
ing marriage and placing it in the context
of God's whole Creation, but it particularly
looks at the effect on women. He's taking
feminists (male and female) at their word
and giving his answer to what they propose,
which is nothing less than a tectonic shift in
human relations—one based on power rather
than love.

You might wish that he would talk directly
to men, and maybe someday there will be

an encyclical about men: Husband, Father, Leader, Protector. I would like to see that.

Our critics can't have it both ways, though—getting upset that everything is about men, and then getting upset that everything is about women.

This is how I read this passage: There is an honor that is specifically reserved for the woman when she bears a child in wedlock, and, given the magnitude of what the sexual act means precisely to the woman—the long-term consequences for her and her child, should she conceive, and the ultimate difference it makes in her life and the lives of her children whether she is married or not. It is only justice to acknowledge that. The difference between man and woman as to the *results* and consequences of childbearing is vast, qualitatively so.

It's a mercy to see the case stated so plainly. The effects of circumlocution are all around us, and I will mention them in a moment. Here I think it's well to acknowledge that it's the woman who suffers most when marriage is torn down, mainly in that a woman who has purposely thrown away her virtue may want to be treated like a woman living in a chaste marriage, but she never will be. She never will be respected (although she may be pitied). This is not so much prescriptive as descriptive, and consulting our own experience will validate the statement.

Second tough bit, speaking about the "trusting obedience which the woman owes to the man."

> Many of them even go further and assert that such a subjection of one party to the other is unworthy of human dignity, that the rights of husband and wife are equal; wherefore, they boldly proclaim the emancipation of women has been or ought to be effected. (74)

and...

> ...for if the woman descends from her truly regal throne to which she has been raised within the walls of the home by means of the Gospel, she will soon be reduced to the old state of slavery (if not in appearance, certainly in reality) and become as amongst the pagans the mere instrument of man. (75)

Don't let your reaction to this one be, at bottom, a question of style, one way or another. The whole notion of submission, or subjection, or obedience – and, conversely of leadership and headship – is not about changing your personality or essential way of grappling with reality.

The problem is that we all have the tendency to confuse *equal* with *same*.

141

So, when, for instance, John Paul II comes along with *Familiaris Consortio* (another important document) and speaks of "mutual subjection," we forget that two people can be equally devoted to each other, but not in an identical way. That "equal in dignity" doesn't mean "equality as sameness."

The wife's being subject to her husband is about two things, one really big thing and one really little thing.

The big thing is that she be willing to go where he goes. As the Irish say, that she hang her washing up with his, that she be buried with his people.

Their relationship won't last long and their children will suffer if an extreme case arises that threatens to separate them, and it can't be resolved by whatever means they normally employ to arrive at an agreement.

The little thing is that she be willing to respect him and to show him that she respects him. I call that one *little* because it has to do with her tone, her attention, and her fundamental bonding to him as a person whose state—not necessarily personality or qualifications—bestow on him the right to be called the head of the family. It's something she gives to him, freely, willingly.

So do you see how those two things are

connected? One big, one little. One macro, one micro, if we can put it that way.

In between is the whole range of human activity and decision-making that can go lots of different ways, depending on how two people are constituted – and that no one, not even Pius XI, is saying anything about *how* you should handle those things.

For the woman, there is a lot of wisdom here, well grounded in Scripture, both in the New Testament and in the Old (see especially Proverbs).

In my experience, women tend to get anxious at the thought that all women should be the same – that some are trying to impose a way of interpreting something on them – that *I* will be forced to go around as quiet as a mouse, never able to speak my mind again!

And that is just not going to happen.

If you are by nature compliant, that's you! True, you might try to be a little more assertive, in charity. But you will not likely change your basic temperament.

If you are by nature someone who pushes back, who speaks out, you might try to soften a little, but you will fundamentally remain the same.

And of course, there's the personality of the husband as well. And then there is the way the two personalities mix. Only God could sort it all out! And He does, by being very encouraging of our freedom, contrary to what most people think.

And the man?

In Scripture, as in these documents, it's abundantly clear that the husband has to be just as devoted as his wife—more so: unto death, the death of Christ on the Cross for His Bride, the Church. He has the task of protecting his wife and his family, regardless of *his* temperament, whether naturally tending to the overtly spirited or not.

The fact is that most men in America are afraid of women, and women in our day have been trained to be, well, obnoxious—specifically towards their husbands. So that is why reading this sort of thing is a good corrective. But you have to know yourself.

And as time goes by in a marriage, experience shows the wisdom of this "division of labor"—husbands love your wives/wives submit to your husbands—because the characteristic fault of the husband is to treat his wife in a loveless manner (even if he really does love her), exerting his power over her, just because exerting power is what he does—and the characteristic fault of the wife is to complain about and boss and nag her husband (and really not to respect him much).

144

A little secret? Wives even sometimes overtly submit to their husbands but in a particularly over-tolerant and uncharitable way! They make their husbands feel stupid, while posing as a submissive wife.

Oh, it's a tricky business! No one wants your submission if that's what it's going to be like!

Be free, be real, be kind.

The same spirit of freedom and devotion goes for the wife working outside the home – or not. Pius XI makes it clear that he is speaking of a social upheaval as an ideology, and circumstances make all the difference. Besides, women have always taken part in outside activities – again, consult Proverbs! A woman to whom God has given say, one child, may have much more opportunity to work outside the home than one who has many children. But, depending on their attitude, each may be equally "enthroned" in her home as its heart and queen – or, sadly, not.

What hurts her state of honor and the honor of marriage itself is when the only thing that counts to society is what her contribution is outside the home, and the warning here is that without serious effort and conviction, it's all too easy for that to be the case.

Society (which after all *is* a community of persons, who are meant to be organized into families) won't descend to seeing women simply as a potential work force and then, ultimately, as just baby-producers on the side — "the mere instrument of man" — unless men and women themselves start to dishonor marriage and the wife's contribution in the home.

That is why Pius XI says this:

> As, however, the social and economic conditions of the married woman must in some way be altered on account of the changes in social intercourse, it is part of the office of the public authority to adapt the civil rights of the wife to modern needs and requirements, keeping in view what the natural disposition and temperament of the female sex, good morality, and the welfare of the family demands, and provided always that the essential order of the domestic society remain intact, founded as it is on something higher than human authority and wisdom, namely on the authority and wisdom of God, and so not changeable by public laws or at the pleasure of private individuals. (77)

Unfortunately, we have more than realized his prophecies. With the never-ending adjustment of the idea of the wife to modern sensibilities, life together isn't working. Feminism (defined here as that which Pius XI is arguing against, the relentless devaluation of the woman's vocation) has led to a war of women against men, with children as the collateral damage.

That can't be. That's why I believe it's worth overcoming our anxieties to find out what God's plan really is, and submit to that, men and women alike.

ADDENDUM TO THIS SECTION

If you find that your discussion of this encyclical is giving rise to lively questions about submission, here is an appendix, to answer two objections, related.

First objection

"Didn't John Paul II override *Casti Connubii* and make the Church's teaching that men and women should submit to each other? Women shouldn't submit to their husbands."

This objection refers to the apostolic exhortation *Familiaris Consortio* (The Role of the Christian Family in the Modern World). It's a beautiful, clear letter that John Paul II wrote with the whole Church and indeed the whole world in mind—including those parts of the world that aren't perhaps always on our mind.

For instance, places where men abuse their natural authority and oppress their wives—

something that Pius XI, in *Casti Connubii*, explicitly forbade.

Where a teaching in one document is based on previous teachings and on Scripture, which the "wives, submit to your husbands" teaching obviously is, it would never and *could never* happen that one pope would "disagree" with another. As Church teaching, an encyclical, which *Casti Connubii* is, ranks higher than an apostolic letter, which *Familiaris Consortio* is. But of course, Scripture ranks highest of all.

But they don't disagree. By looking at the footnotes of *Familiaris Consortio*, we can see that it too is based on Scripture and, mainly, *Humanae Vitae*, the encyclical on marital relations that came after *Casti Connubii*. *Humanae Vitae*, in turn, is based on *Casti Connubii* (which in turn rests on *Arcanum*, a document from Pope Leo XIII, also well worth reading).

Any papal document is based on Scripture, tradition, and right reason. And there is no denying that Scripture says that a man must love his wife as Christ loved the Church (unto death), and a wife must submit (or obey) her husband. (Ephesians 5:22–33, Colossians 3:18, 19)

Each pope tries to take into consideration the needs of his people and the whole world at the time and then explain things accordingly. Both Pius XI and John Paul II tried to do this, and naturally they have different emphases.

One way to think of what is said about mutual subjection in *Familiaris Consortio* is this: Each must be subject to the other in accordance with God's plan and with his or her own characteristic strengths and weaknesses – and above all, with the good of the family – in mind. We must also refrain from making the mistake of thinking that "mutual subjection" means "uniformly subjected" or "subjected in the same way." Taking into consideration the differences between man and woman, we ought to recognize that their subjection would have different manifestations. John Paul left this to be worked out by the two, in the light of the teachings of the past and of the words of the Bible.

For our part, we are often so blinded by the ideology of equality (as sameness, rejecting complementarity) that we don't acknowledge the damage done when the principle of Scripture and of the authentic teaching of the Church is not followed – when we condition Scripture to our own time and place, denying its universal character. So, for instance, we fail to do what popes must do, which is to see the universal application of their teachings.

For instance, a critic might not consider that a wife might receive a job offer so enticing that she would leave her family to pursue it. But that does happen in our world. And that is what Pius XI presciently foretold. He was the

149

pope of the alpha female of corporate America just as much as the pope of the burqa'd Afghani woman – regardless of whether either of these poor unfortunates realizes it or not.

This might help, from the incomparable William May of the John Paul II Institute (it's worth reading the whole article):

> In speaking of the mutual submission of husbands and wives to each other out of love for Christ, John Paul II, as Germain Grisez has properly noted and discussed at length, in no way rejected the tradition represented by Pope Pius XI. The different papal teachings are compatible. As Grisez points out, Pius XI, while admonishing wives to obey their husbands, was careful to emphasize that a husband must respect his wife's equal personal dignity and should not dominate her, because she is equal in dignity to her husband. John Paul II, stressing the obligation of spouses to submit mutually to one another in Christ, notes that male domination of women is the result of the latter's vulnerability and of original sin. But at the same time he emphasizes the "specific diversity and personal originality of man and

woman." Women rightly resist dom-
ination, but in doing so they must
not, he says, become "masculinized"
and "appropriate to themselves male
characteristics contrary to their own
feminine originality." By affirming
the difference between men and
women John Paul II implies the
legitimacy of sexually differentiated
roles in marriage. Although he does
not spell these out, either in *Mulieris
Dignitatem* or in *Familiaris Consortio*, he affirms, as I have stressed,
that the husband/father has a leadership (headship) role within the
family, and the implication is that
this role requires of the husband/
father a unique kind of authority
within the family.[2]

Second objection

"Sometimes men aren't really interested in
having a wife subject to them."

This state of affairs, where men decline to be
leaders, can come about for various reasons.
They may interpret "submission" in a cultur-
ally indefensible way, they may not make the
distinction between submission owed to their

2 William May, "The Mission of Fatherhood: 'To
Reveal and Relive on Earth the Very Fatherhood of
God' (cf. *Familiaris consortio* 25)," at christendom-awake.
org/pages/may/father.

state as leader of the family as opposed to subjection to their personal whims, and they may be afraid to claim rightful submission based on the hierarchy of the family.

John Paul spoke of "mutual subjection" because, of course, both should show respect to each other.

In our pervasive feminist culture, I'd like to make the following observation.

The wife particularly needs to show respect in her everyday dealings with her husband *precisely* because she does make most of the day-to-day decisions and in fact is competent with the myriad details – and easily falls into the habit of issuing orders to husband and children alike.

For years that can work, but when a rough patch arises, the husband suffers from feeling bossed and feeling that his opinion isn't important to his wife. Not in the first decade, maybe, but later. For this reason, the couple finds that raising their children into adulthood becomes almost unbearably stressful.

The wife can make most of the decisions with a subtle scorn for her husband, or her attitude can be loving kindness. Some women are good at being kind and supportive and positive. In a different culture, the women who are not good at it would have some formation to fall back on. In ours, women as a group tend to affirm everyone but their husbands.

Many somewhat spirited women, those who can't help objecting to the "submission" teaching, perhaps take for granted a certain basic submission that they already have, namely, the submission to the plan.

For instance, if this sort of woman's husband got a job in another place, she would go with him. She might perhaps argue and plead and cry, but in the end, she agrees – she consents – that the ultimate decision is his, for the sake of the family. A man needs to know that his wife will go with him wherever he has to go, in spirit as well as in body. In a way, you could say that the burden is on him, because the blame is on him if he fails to protect her and their family.

Her submission is to their unity. It is not, as some Protestants teach, to the obliteration of her own personhood. His headship is in doing what needs to be done to protect his family and provide for his loved ones.

The sort of outcry against *this* sort of submission – her willingness to submit to their unity, under his headship – is the "equality" Pius XI speaks against.

7

Three ways the family is the school of justice and mercy

The question for the woman in our day becomes, "If I devote myself to my family, will I be failing to offer help and mercy to others outside the home?" In a way you could say that this question sparked my determination to produce a contemporary gloss on *Casti Connubii*.

If we agree with the premise of the encyclical in principle, the challenge seems to be that if women raise their own children, even willing to suffer the conditions in our society at present of isolation and lack of affirmation, what will happen to the world of people who need ministering to?

Here are three thoughts, based on the reading of *Casti Connubii* (as well as *Familiaris Consortio* and *Mulieris Dignitatem*).

1. Living together in harmony, the family teaches the virtue of justice.

The structure of the family offers a model of what we could call *applied justice*. John Paul II kept repeating that the world passes through the family.

Each person passes by way of the family.

Because the family, even when imperfect, *by its nature* is a sanctuary of the weak (what is weaker than an infant?), it offers love to those whose only claim to be taken care of is just that they exist.

In itself, this is a lesson for humanity in justice. But when the family fulfills its role as teacher and "first school of virtue," then we see how justice is learned. And how else could it be learned? You must learn these things at your parents' knees or have a rough road ahead of you.

Justice is the virtue of giving everyone his due.

The family offers justice to the child, because it protects and nurtures the child before sending him out into the world. A child needs stability almost more than anything else (which is why good societies always try to make it the last resort to take a child away, even from a bad family, but rather give the family the help it needs if possible). A baby is so vulnerable that, in the normal course of things, only by having two committed parents can the child really survive and thrive.

The family offers justice to the woman, because bearing a child is a risky business. The family offers the wife *protection* when she's at her most vulnerable and *affirmation* of the need to have time to bond with her baby. Only in a family can a woman properly nurture her children! Through life, the family recognizes her contribution and doesn't abandon her in her old age, when she is through with her productive years. Instead, it crowns her with honor for her sacrifice. This is why motherhood should never be separated from the family, why a woman's childbearing gift must never be exploited.

The family offers justice to the man, who, without this bond, would not have a strong enough connection to his wife and his children. When a man gives his all for his family, working for them, protecting them, his contributions are honored and his loved ones stay close to him. It would be unjust to view a man as detachable from the good of the family.

So when men, women, and children live in families, they are experiencing justice and providing justice to others. This justice spreads, because as they gather in a community and the communities form the state, everyone has a stake in doing what is best for the least powerful among them and giving everyone his due, which is justice.

2. The family daily lives out mercy.

The family may not be taking in beggars from the streets (or it may), but when you are washing your children's feet, cleaning their little bottoms, and nursing them, you are doing acts of mercy. The mother of Jesus did all these things, and she was the most virtuous human being ever created.

If you do it for the least of these, you did it for Me, Jesus said.

If a woman leaves the house to feed half-a-dozen children in an orphanage, will she feel more holy than when she feeds her own children? That's a little misguided. If a woman leaves her house to teach catechism to strangers' children, is she more holy than when she sits on the sofa and reads a Bible story to her own?

When a man lifts his child up to reach something he needs, he is showing mercy. When he encourages his older boys to help the younger children, he is teaching mercy. When a man cares gently for his wife when she is sick, he is merciful and just.

3. This mercy within the family very quickly begins to overflow into the world at large.

I remember, years ago when I was a busy young mother, a friend who had just had a baby thanked me for a dinner I brought. She said that it was only her friends with many young children who had thought to do it; her less encumbered friends offered her nothing. So even when the children are little, the strong family still looks out for others in a practical way, precisely because of what they are experiencing.

It's true that in the first few years of a family's life, normally the activity is very much focused inward. Fortunately, families are all at different stages of development! So while your little family is learning to take care of itself, so to speak, others are growing outwards, taking in those in need, rescuing the poor, organizing relief. The day comes when life isn't all getting babies from one point in the day to the other, and your gaze turns to those in need, even as new little families are just learning the ways of caring for the babies in their midst.

4. Without the family, we'd have no way to offer very much to the poor.

There would be very little productivity on the economic level, because people work for the sake of families and are creative because they have leisure afforded by their families.

There would be very few volunteers, because volunteers are the fruit of families — people whose support has been provided by someone else and have free time to offer to others.

There wouldn't even be religious orders, because, apart from Divine intervention, the virtue necessary to make the sacrifice to live as a religious is normally learned in the family! It's well known that most military special forces operatives, religious, and even college resident assistants come from large families! Generous family life teaches people to help others.

When a child has the misfortune of lacking a parent, his extended family or another generous family steps in to provide. When a mother is abandoned, her community – of families – helps her.

If there are children living next door whose single mom doesn't come home until late, well, it's the neighbor family who makes sure they have a snack and get their homework done. Where there is no neighbor family, the children next door are lonely.

Even the increasingly extolled value of free, unrestricted play for children – play where they can roam unsupervised, making their own rules and having their own adventures, yet in safety – relies utterly on the existence of families and particularly mothers and other "unproductive" persons being home.

And it's worth taking a moment to think about what life was like when women primarily stayed home. Far from being selfish, self-seeking spoiled narcissists, or beneficiaries of "privilege," hard-working women created a network of community support that made it so that children were free to run around and learn in safety and old people were cared for at home, rather than left in loneliness in nursing homes. Who has time to visit the elderly when everyone works?

I think that often we compare the richest people of today with the poorest of other eras, rather than thinking about how the poor fare today. In other words, when we think of single moms, we think of the ones we read about in glossy magazines who are single by choice, not the ones using food stamps at the checkout. We don't really dwell on what it's like to have sick children and no options. We don't try to visualize being postpartum with no husband to take care of a plumbing emergency. We take for granted that these situations can be met by paying someone to handle them, but that is rarely true.

And when we forget that a family is uniquely qualified to deal with a bunch of children with the flu right there at home, we end up with expensive and inept schemes for the government to provide care – or, increasingly, we just send sick kids to school. Is it any wonder that the flu spreads so readily? Everyone is compelled to go out when they are sick!

I'm sure many more examples can be added to this list of how families administer justice and mercy to the world.

Families fill in to offer what's needed in the brokenness around them, and where necessary, form associations to help those on a larger scale, but still with the compassion of personal relationship. Thus we see the principle of subsidiarity put into practice, with those nearest the problem doing their best to take care of it.

Now we're seeing that as the family gets redefined, the government steps in. But the family is actually an amazingly efficient delivery system for social good at the source, where the government is a clumsy, expensive, inefficient, wasteful, and at best, patchy, remedy at the other end.

One of the most important elements to providing needed help is *information*, and clearly those nearest to the problem have the best information about it. This experience confirms the Catholic principle of subsidiarity: the further you get from the problem, the less effective, the less *just*, becomes the remedy.

Committing to the family as God's plan is the way to start healing our society!

Before you know it, your own family will be the hub of good works in your community. As you join with others in solidarity, your family will become one of many hubs, all doing good in God's kingdom.

8

What we do "in here"
(94–end)

I fear that I won't do our reading justice, because the subject is so vast. With marriage, where to begin with the finishing of the discussion?

Should we start with the government, with the subject of justice towards those who commit themselves to raising families? After all, families are what government seeks (or ought to seek) to protect.

Should we start with married people, who may or may not realize that if they don't commit themselves to the family, rather than to some sort of self-fulfillment project, will end up with children who, in their turn, don't know how to undertake their responsibilities?

Should we start with the clergy, whom we would like somehow to convince that it's their job to interpret Revelation and learn the wisdom of the Church handed down in documents such as *Casti Connubii*, passing it on to ordinary people?

Should we start with the children, so that they can overcome their parents' mistakes and confusion, rescuing the world from chaos?

Casti Connubii ends with recommendations for action, and basically, the answer is, all of the above.

First, the Church needs to preach the truth about God's plan for man: His first covenant with the first couple, that they become one flesh, so that their union of love be the cradle of humanity.

It's up to bishops and priests to teach this, but don't hold your breath on that one. History shows that the bishops, in particular, won't be a lot of help, starting with St. Peter that fateful night when he couldn't admit to a serving maid that he knew Our Lord.

Still, it could happen that a priest would be willing to read this encyclical, for instance, with you, and that would be a good thing. (105) Consider hosting a reading group that includes any willing clergy.

Second, the whole world needs reforming (117) so that it is properly ordered to this most fundamental of human relationships, marriage, and governments claim or reclaim their role in serving justice, which means, serving the person in his weakest manifestation. What you and I can do about that at the moment,

I think is limited, to say the least.

We do what we can.

But in between these two recommendations, from paragraphs 110 to 116, is a very heartfelt and elemental plea that families themselves *simply understand the importance of what they do – of what we do.*

And this should give us a lot of hope, because we can't get a bishop to do anything at all, and our government is barreling along without us, but we can do something about our very own home and our very own children!

God, it turns out, didn't order the world so that if you aren't the President you are helpless. He didn't order reality so that if you don't have earthly power, you are pretty much sunk.

He did the opposite. He confounded the wise. (I Corinthians 1:27) He made the littlest things of the utmost importance.

He made reality so that a man who humbly does a sort of unpleasant job for the sake of his family is in fact the real lord of the manor, with many dependents (ones he may never see or meet in this world) and much fruitfulness. A man of no account in the world of law-making or no voice in the even more important world of preaching and spiritual leadership can yet be the builder of a rich culture and the sower of prosperous fields.

If you don't really think this is true and real—that it is actually His plan to use the weak to confound the mighty—then you will miss precisely what it is you say you seek—a way to do important things!

This is the key to understanding how it is that a woman's call to love the little place of her home is such a great and even momentous action in the world—if you have ears to hear it. If you can love the hidden and resist the lure of the oversized and loud and lucrative claim to fame, you will have the privilege to know how it can be that one woman, one family, one home—yours—can change and build and restore.

In (112 and 113) especially, we have strong reminders of the bad things that happen if we neglect to have a good home and the good things that will happen if we try to have a good home.

> God wills that . . . the father be truly a father, and the mother truly a mother; through their devout love and unwearying care, the home, though it suffer the want and hardship of this valley of tears, may become for the children in its own way a foretaste of that paradise of delight in which the Creator placed the first men of the human race. Thus will they be able to bring up

their children as perfect men and perfect Christians; they will instill into them a sound understanding of the Catholic Church, and will give them such a disposition and love for their fatherland as duty and gratitude demand. (113)

All the things of the earth: The state ("their fatherland"), the Church (the spiritual community), and the person in his context of the family—all these depend on how things are lived in the home—and what the children are taught by their devoted parents.

Because, as we keep repeating, the whole of humanity, every person, passes through the family, God willing, on his or her way to heaven.

9

Final note

I know that the question of *how* – how to live this family life (even in "want and hardship" as Pius XI puts it) – is the burning question, once we've gone and made the commitment. (Occasionally, the reverse happens: Devoted mothers and fathers live the little things well and then realize they've gone and built themselves a good life. What a blessing!)

I can remember sitting with my baby and basically saying, "The spirit is willing but the flesh has no idea how to proceed." Thus began many years of re-inventing that particular wheel, and many tears of frustration at my own ignorance.

And so, dear reader, that is why our blog, *Like Mother, Like Daughter,* exists, which is what I reminded myself when I first wrote these words there, and was wondering how to end on a practical note.

My work there has been to try to answer the question, "What now?" on the theory that what really matters is what we do "in here," in family life; and to offer as many ways and means of living that life as I can. I hope you will seek us out on our site.

My thought for you, as I read this encyclical and wonder just what dear old Pius XI would think of the state of things today, prophetic as he was, is the same as my thought for me: Let's take our sweet Lord at His word, and have faith in His covenant of marriage.

"He who has hope lives differently."
— Pope Benedict XVI

APPENDIX 1

Examining
Amoris Laetitia ¶298 in
Light of *Casti Connubii* ¶10

When I had finished and published as a Kindle book the preceding "guided reading," I came back to paragraph 10 of *Casti Connubii*, as the world's bishops settled into acceptance of what Pope Francis's Apostolic Exhortation *Amoris Laetitia* teaches. The stark contrast between the conclusions of St. Augustine on one hand and Pope Francis on the other led me to the following analysis.[1]

Now that we have delved into the encyclical's teaching on the nature of marriage in our reading and are convinced of the immutability of the institution of marriage and the family, let's bring its teaching to bear on today's confusion.

---

1   I am indebted to the authors of the *"Letter to Cardinal Angelo Sodano, Dean of the College of Cardinals,"* 29th June, 2016, for the observation about the problematic footnote to the paragraph of *Amoris Laetitia* in question.

CHANGE OR CONTINUITY?

Amoris Laetitia ("The Joy of Love"), Pope Francis' apostolic exhortation on marriage, was promulgated immediately after the second Synod on the Family in 2016. At its release, many strove to absorb its lengthy contents; many who had been anxious during the synod proceedings expressed confusion or outright dismay; many were silent.

Some bishops (Cardinals Müller, Wuerl, Farrell, and Cupich, to name a few) and bishops' conferences (for instance those of Malta and Germany) presented the exhortation to the faithful in their regions as a legitimate development of doctrine, one that addresses discipline or pastoral understanding and not the principles of the moral law itself.

Some popular commentators (for instance Stephen Walford in Vatican Insider and Eric Scott Alt and David Anderson on their blogs) further argued and continue to argue that development of doctrine can only be defined by the pope himself; they hold that whatever he teaches is by its nature, as *his* teaching, development and not departure from Tradition, and that, in Walford's words,

> We must affirm that Pope Francis cannot possibly be in error in his ordinary magisterium concerning issues of faith and morals, and thus

his teaching [in *Amoris Laetitia*] that under certain, carefully considered cases, Holy Communion can be given to person in irregular situations is perfectly valid and influenced by the Holy Spirit.

We continue to see this sanguine acceptance of new statements from the Vatican and defenses of them with the change in the Catechism of the Catholic Church on the subjects of capital punishment and the unique salvation offered by Jesus Christ.

Is this line of defense true? Ought the faithful to accept every new teaching as a valid development?

In his work defending the "substantial unity" of the deposit of faith, *An Essay on the Development of Christian Doctrine*, Blessed John Henry Newman explained how a new teaching can be weighed. He posited that any teaching must be

one in type, one in its system of principles, one in its unitive power towards externals, one in its logical consecutiveness, one in the witness of its early phases to its later, one in the protection which its later extend to its earlier, and one in its vigor with continuance, that is, in its tenacity.

This test allows the ordinary Catholic, who, by virtue of his baptism, must hold the creed "a treasure to transmit" (in Newman's words in his striking sermon, *The Gospel, A Trust Committed to Us*) to assure himself that those entrusted with the teaching office of the Church, the Magisterium, have remained constant to the truth. The ordinary Christian, to put it bluntly, must take care that he is not being misled, or others are not being misled, into assenting to a message that breaks from what has been taught in the past, going right back to the Gospel –due to bad will, sloppy work, faulty interpretation, or failure to recognize distinctions in levels of magisterial authority.

When we look at history and Revelation, we see that the truth is knowable. Jesus Christ, who is the Truth, and His teachings are accessible to His followers. Truth is not the exclusive domain of academics and theologians only; these experts can aid us in understanding, but cannot ultimately claim exclusive sovereignty over, matters of faith and morals – of the knowledge of those things. The Gospel itself assures us:

> In the same hour Jesus rejoiced in spirit and said, I praise thee, Father, Lord of the heaven and of the earth, that thou hast hid these things from wise and prudent, and hast revealed them to babes: yea, Father, for thus

> has it been well-pleasing in thy
> sight. (Luke 10:21)

In short, an ordinary faithful Catholic can read an exhortation about marriage and be able at least to say that it does not make sense in light of the Gospel. He may not know *where* it goes wrong, but he can at least know that it *does* go wrong. He can at least ask for clarification so that he may be shown that it does not go wrong.

With this reminder of our legitimate duty as baptized Christians, let's look at Paragraph 10 of *Casti Connubii*, the encyclical on marriage written by Pius XI in 1930. Of the magisterial documents that deal with marriage, this one delves most deeply into its nature as well as its challenges, carefully enlarging upon previous teachings and Scripture. The encyclical examines the relationship between husband and wife and wrestles in a prophetic way with the results of abandoning marriage in its nature and as Sacrament.

Paragraph 10 lays out the blessings of marriage, and it ends with the following quote from St. Augustine:

> By conjugal faith it is provided that there should be no carnal intercourse outside the marriage bond with another man or woman; with regard to offspring, that children

should be begotten of love, tenderly cared for and educated in a religious atmosphere; finally, in its sacramental aspect that the marriage bond should not be broken and that a husband or wife, if separated, should not be joined to another even for the sake of offspring. This we regard as the law of marriage by which the fruitfulness of nature is adorned and the evil of incontinence is restrained. (CC 10)

This paragraph contains an important point—the duty of the separated—that has been missed in the inquiry of our present time as to the nature and problem of marriage and adultery in *Amoris Laetitia* (AL).

FAMILIARIS CONSORTIO

There are other points of contention with AL, most famously with the five *Dubia* (questions for clarification) presented by four cardinals to Pope Francis.[2] These respectful questions, which center on Paragraphs 300–305, have not yet, at this writing, been answered.

The arguments contained in the *Dubia* and the paragraphs they focus on are obviously in good hands with the remaining two cardinals

---

2   These cardinals were Raymond Burke, Walter Brandmüller, Carlo Caffarra, and Joachim Meisner.

(Meisner and Caffarra having passed away since the *Dubia* were presented). I propose instead, invoking my baptismal promise, to examine a different paragraph of AL to see how it relates to the section from *Casti Connubii* (CC) that I quoted above. I am interested in this portion of Paragraph 298 of AL:

> The divorced who have entered a new union, for example, can find themselves in a variety of situations, which should not be pigeonholed or fit into overly rigid classifications leaving no room for a suitable personal and pastoral discernment. One thing is a second union consolidated over time, with new children, proven fidelity, generous self giving, Christian commitment, a consciousness of its irregularity and of the great difficulty of going back without feeling in conscience that one would fall into new sins. The Church acknowledges situations "where, for serious reasons, such as the children's upbringing, a man and woman cannot satisfy the obligation to separate." (*Amoris Laetitia* 298)

Let's look at this language carefully, because it represents a departure from the technical way that popes have spoken about moral issues in the past, using precise language in order to avoid confusion. AL instead employs a more affective and emotive idiom that may prove to elide or blur some important concepts.

Here Pope Francis posits a somewhat vaguely defined situation (that "over time," with "proven fidelity," this second union has come to resemble marriage), in which the serious reasons of the children's upbringing are presumed to make impossible or difficult what St. Augustine and Pius XI call the *obligatory* separation of the "irregular" couple.

The very way the hypothetical situation is presented, with its imputation of the couple's virtue ("proven fidelity," "generous self giving," etc.) and dearth of objective criteria as to their exact conjugal relationship, makes criticism here seem unworthy; all the moral weight seems to be on the side of this new relationship, without any real explanation, other than that time has passed and feelings have changed — circumstances that are not possible to verify but which serve to bolster the claim.

As we read any papal document, we must remember that its gravity and truth depend on its preservation of and grounding in what the Catechism of the Catholic Church calls the "supremely wise arrangement of God": The Sacred Magisterium, Sacred Tradition, and Sacred Scripture. *On this continuity* — and not on the seeming reasonableness of its declarations apart from the continuity – depends the validity and, as Newman is at pains to repeat, the *unity* of the teaching. The unity of the teaching is the seal of its validity.

St. Vincent of Lérins, a fifth-century monk often cited when the topic arises of the necessity of doctrinal exposition, provides Newman the basis for characterizing authentic development:

> Let there be growth and abundant progress in understanding, knowledge, and wisdom, in each and all, in individuals and in the whole Church, at all times and in the progress of ages, *but only with the proper limits, i.e., within the same dogma, the same meaning, the same judgment.*[3]

With these criteria in mind, let's go back to CC: in Paragraph 10 quoted above, Pope Pius XI cites St. Augustine to explain the goods of marriage. To preserve the sacred character of marriage, so vital to the flourishing of human life, "a husband or wife, if separated, should not be joined to another *even for the sake of offspring.*" I add emphasis to show how pointed and concise Augustine's comment is, as if no argument is needed for so plain a value, *the sanctity of the bond.*

---

3 Emphasis added.

St. John Paul II, in his apostolic exhortation *Familiaris Consortio*, written in 1981 as an expression of that era's synod of bishops on marriage and its difficulties, addressed the issue of divorce and remarriage further, clearly grappling with the need to offer the perennial teaching of the Church to a modern and confused world.

Now, I have seen many references to *Familiaris Consortio* (FC) in the discussion in our day regarding *Amoris Laetitia* and its ambiguities; but I am not aware of an argument that puts the two — John Paul II's FC and Francis' AL — in context with *Casti Connubii*. Yet, I suggest that this is a necessary triangulation. It will disclose the moral geography of the question in light of the whole body of Church teaching, rooted in Tradition and Sacred Scripture — that is, a triangulation that reveals the preservation of unity insisted on by Newman — or the lack thereof.

There was no question that by 1981, the year *Familiaris Consortio* was promulgated, the warnings of Pius XI had come to pass, and society had changed considerably. More and more families were in objectively immoral situations, just as he had predicted would happen. Those situations needed to be addressed from a pastoral point of view, to help those to whom the Gospel had been preached. The world is full of people; the imagination is beggared by the possible number of exceptional circumstances. *Familiaris Consortio* acknowledges this:

> Daily experience unfortunately shows that people who have obtained a divorce usually intend to enter into a new union, obviously not with a Catholic religious ceremony. Since this is an evil that, like the others, is affecting more and more Catholics as well, the problem must be faced with resolution and without delay. The Synod Fathers studied it expressly. The Church, which was set up to lead to salvation all people and especially the baptized, cannot abandon to their own devices those who have been previously bound by sacramental marriage and who have attempted a second marriage. The Church will therefore make untiring efforts to put at their disposal her means of salvation. (*Familiaris Consortio* 84)

Teaching, however, must deal with principles. It must offer precepts that can be consulted to apply right action in particular circumstances. John Paul laid down the criteria for those couples to return to reception of the Eucharist:

> Reconciliation in the sacrament of Penance which would open the way to the Eucharist, can only be granted

to those who, repenting of having broken the sign of the Covenant and of fidelity to Christ, are sincerely ready to undertake a way of life that is no longer in contradiction to the indissolubility of marriage. This means, in practice, that when, for serious reasons, such as for example the children's upbringing, a man and a woman cannot satisfy the obligation to separate, they "take on themselves the duty to live in complete continence, that is, by abstinence from the acts proper to married couples." (*Familiaris Consortio* 84)

CDF CLARIFICATIONS

This teaching, one that did not contradict what went before it, but *did* attempt to take into consideration new situations, was further clarified by the Congregation for the Doctrine of the Faith (CDF), the office of the Vatican that has the duty to promulgate, defend, and clarify doctrinal issues. Then-Cardinal Joseph Ratzinger (the future Pope Benedict XVI), prefect of the congregation at the time, elaborated on whether the divorced and remarried can receive Holy Communion, or whether such reception constitutes the sin of adultery.

Pastors in some places were allowing divorced and remarried people to approach Holy

Communion after finding that they had examined their conscience and felt it to have authorized them to do so. The CDF document asserted against this position that we must "recall the doctrine and discipline of the Church in this matter."

> The faithful who persist in such a situation [the remarriage] may receive Holy Communion only after obtaining sacramental absolution, which may be given only "to those who, repenting of having broken the sign of the Covenant and of fidelity to Christ, are sincerely ready to undertake a way of life that is no longer in contradiction to the indissolubility of marriage. This means, in practice, that when for serious reasons, for example, for the children's upbringing, a man and a woman *cannot satisfy the obligation to separate*, they 'take on themselves the duty to live in complete continence, that is, by abstinence from the acts proper to married couples.'" In such a case they may receive Holy Communion as long as they respect the obligation to avoid giving scandal.[4]

---

4 Letter to the Bishops Concerning the Reception of Holy Communion by the Divorced and Remarried Members of the Faithful, ¶4, emphasis mine.

The words I have emphasized, "the obligation to separate," recall the words in *Casti Connubii,* Paragraph 10 cited above: "a husband or wife, if separated, should not be joined to another [implying that if they are joined, they must separate] even for the sake of offspring."

Cardinal Ratzinger further brings to mind in particular the point that receiving Communion depends on abstaining not only from sexual relations but even from the *appearance* of having relations, which would give scandal concerning the sacramental nature of marriage. This idea of scandal—a behavior or attitude that leads someone else into sin—is important to include in the discussion, because the good of society depends on marriage being honored by the person and by society in its three attributes: Fidelity, Children, and Sacrament (these attributes are discussed in chapter two of this volume).

Cardinal Ratzinger goes on to explain why "the value of the new union" cannot be determined by conscience alone: "Marriage is ... essentially a public reality" (¶7).

The whole of *Casti Connubii*—indeed, the whole body of Church teaching on marriage up until AL—brings this truth to light and builds the entire edifice of our life here on earth upon it: our personal, political, and economic relationships, which all are grounded in this primordial institution.

Marriage is a public state that exists to transform the created world and to bring it to God; it is certainly the necessary condition for an orderly society even as a natural institution; and Cardinal Ratzinger says in his Letter that it is a "reality of the Church, that is to say, a sacrament" (¶8).

Marriage exists for the salvation of souls: husband, wife, and especially the souls of the children born into it. In fact, the original plan of God for children is that they be brought to Him by means of the institution of marriage. That is the origin of the old adage that God has no grandchildren, only children: "For you are all the children of God by faith in Christ Jesus" (Gal 3: 26). God's plan is that each person learns his childhood in God, in the family.

The question is simple: whether *Amoris Laetitia* ¶298 (among others), in fact represents a *discontinuity* rather than an organic development, precisely by leveraging this importance of the well being of children in the posited new "marriage" – to *justify* its existence, when *Casti Connubii* 10 *explicitly rejects this condition.*

CC perhaps surprises the reader of our age by asserting that the couple in an illicit arrangement must separate and cannot use the children as a rationale for remaining together in a new coupling. I would argue that it's so surprising that we simply gloss over it in its brevity. Yet, FC references the obligation as so fundamental that no citation is needed (nor can one be found, in CC, FC, the CDF documents, or elsewhere, as far as I know; it seems to be as pure a given as you will find). Yet in AL, somehow, *without argument*, as if it is self-evident, the implicit excuse is offered precisely "for the sake of the children," as a reason to *overlook* the previous divorce and *not separate*.

This is of course the opposite of what *Casti Connubii* says.

THE SACRAMENTAL SYSTEM

But what about this very principle, of marriage existing for the purpose of sheltering children? Perhaps we ought to accept the new attitude expressed in AL because it makes more sense when held up to the goods of the sacrament, which, as *Casti Connubii* reminds us, include children. Isn't it the case that the children will suffer material and even emotional hardship if the parents separate? Especially if the separation is because of a condition from the past that they consider no longer relevant to their lives?

What Cardinal Ratzinger argues in the Letter from the CDF is that the objective nature of the sacrament must be preserved—that is, that no action can be taken that gives the lie to its reality; that it isn't a convenience or a mere contract, but a public act for the good of society (above all for children, who are most vulnerable) and for the salvation of souls.

Implicit in what he says is that children, deep in their formation as persons, will assimilate the wrong idea about marriage if this objective reality is contradicted. On a fundamental level, adults, in docility to this teaching power of the Church, must give witness to the covenant and the One who made it, even if the witness requires sacrifice, for the noble reason that the continued understanding of the Church's mission is at stake. Undermine one sacrament and the whole sacramental system crumbles.

Of course, the Church does not want a child to go hungry or be without a roof over his head. She asks that, if this is the case, the couple then live together as brother and sister (provided, as Ratzinger elaborates, they can do this without giving the impression that they are married – that is, causing scandal).

Perhaps the modern difficulty of requiring the seemingly impossible sacrifice of sexual relations stems from the neglect of even our most outspoken orthodox theologians and prelates to advert to any document on marriage before *Familiaris Consortio*. Even the *Dubia* fail to reference *Casti Connubii*, its predecessor *Arcanum*, or any other document that predates even the 20th century.

MISLEADING FOOTNOTES

In *Amoris Laetitia* itself, in the section under contention, even the relevant passage from FC is footnoted only partially, not in its entirety, and the portion reproduced omits the important clause that goes on to reject admission to Holy Communion for the divorced and remarried—the very clause that keeps it squarely in continuity with previous teaching—the very clause that touches on the question that the waiting world considered the most important in AL!

This footnote (329) seems to use previous teachings to reinforce the idea of a new and approved bond that keeps the couple in communion with the Church; the citations provide credence for the substance of the paragraph two which they relate.

But we must be careful, because the wording makes the conclusion seem to originate in the citation; but it is added to it by an unknown voice, and then elided with another citation. This assertion will take unpacking, so please bear with me as we look at this footnote:

> 329 John Paul II, Apostolic Exhortation *Familiaris Consortio* (22 November 1981), 84: AAS 74 (1982), 186. In such situations, many people, knowing and accepting the possibility of living "as brothers and sisters"

which the Church offers them, point
out that if certain expressions of
intimacy are lacking, "it often happens that faithfulness is endangered
and the good of the children suffers"
(Second Vatican Ecumenical Council,
Pastoral Constitution on the Church
in the Modern World *Gaudium et
Spes*, 51).

The bolded words do *not* appear in *Familiaris
Consortio*, although they are placed in a way
to suggest that they are a paraphrase. Nor are
they related to the words in quote marks that
follow. They represent an unattributed voice
in the document.

The Vatican II constitution *Guadium et Spes*
paragraph 51 does indeed speak of the difficulties "where the intimacy of married life
is broken off, its faithfulness can sometimes
be imperiled and its quality of fruitfulness
ruined, for then the upbringing of the children and the courage to accept new ones are
both endangered." But this passage occurs in
the context of *validly married couples* and the
necessity of honoring the moral law regarding
the transmission of life and rejecting abortion and artificial contraception. In short, the
Council here does not speak about divorce and
remarriage at all; it is not addressing "irregular situations." The words from *Guadium et
Spes* have no relevance to the subject.

This footnote, using a strange compression and even sleight of hand, has the effect of rendering the paragraph (298) to which it is attached to be the opposite of the actual teaching of FC and of CC before it.[5]

THE WITNESS OF SCRIPTURE AND THE MAGISTERIUM

Not even the words of Our Lord Himself on the topic of divorce merit a mention in the section of *Amoris Laetitia* we are examining—for instance, Mark 10:11–12: "Whoever divorces his wife and marries another, commits adultery against her; and if she divorces her husband and marries another, she commits adultery." And it is hardly necessary to say that nowhere in this synodal document do we find any reference to the CDF's subsequent

---

5   Even further confusion results from an old article of Ratzinger's from 1972, when he was professor at the University of Regensburg. His conclusions at that time (which precedes his prefecture at the CDF, during which he adhered strictly to the norms regulating Holy Communion for the divorced and remarried) track closely to those of *Amoris Laetitia* in some ways. Cardinal Kasper of Germany dredged the article up in preparation for the synod. A treatment of this episode, including Benedict's formal retraction of his original statements, can be found in an article entitled *In the Synod on the Family: Even the Pope Emeritus Is Speaking Out*, by Sandro Magister, found on his site chiesa. espresso.repubblica.it, Dec. 3, 2014, and reported on by Catholic News Agency, Dec. 4, 2014, "*Ratzinger's retraction: the fruit of 42 years of theological maturation.*"

clarification and reinforcement of Pope John
Paul's teaching that I have outlined here.

Paragraph 298 of *Amoris Laetitia*, departing
from the usual vocabulary used when speaking of the sacrament of marriage, calls it "the
ideal which the Gospel proposes for marriage
and the family... *We know that no 'easy recipes'
exist.*"[6]

The word "ideal" does not occur in *Casti
Connubii* or *Humanae Vitae*. It does however
appear in *Familiaris Consortio* – to be *rejected*
in favor of something more concrete:

> [Married people] cannot however
> look on the law as merely an *ideal*
> to be achieved in the future: they
> must consider it as a command of
> Christ the Lord to overcome diffi-
> culties with constancy. "And so what
> is known as 'the law of gradualness'
> or step-by-step advance cannot
> be identified with 'gradualness of
> the law,' as if there were different
> degrees or forms of precept in God's
> law for different individuals and sit-
> uations. In God's plan, all husbands
> and wives are called in marriage
> to holiness, and this lofty vocation
> is fulfilled to the extent that the
> human person is able to respond to

---

6   Emphasis added.

God's command with serene confidence in God's grace and in his or her own will."[7]

With only a partial reference to FC and none at all to *Casti Connubii*, we see how a distorted, unbalanced teaching or interpretation has arisen in dioceses around the world, subsequent to the promulgation of *Amoris Laetitia*, and how confusion has taken hold. Even Cardinal Schönborn, designated by Pope Francis as his functional interpreter for the purposes of the exhortation, in his interview with Fr. Antonio Spadaro left the impression that Cardinal Ratzinger of the CDF agreed with Pope Francis as to the possibility of the "interior forum" settling the question of Communion for the divorced and remarried:

> I remember asking Cardinal Ratzinger in 1994, when the Congregation for the Doctrine of the Faith had published its document about divorced and remarried persons: "Is it possible that the old praxis that was taken for granted, and that I knew before the [Second Vatican] Council, is still valid? This envisaged the possibility, in the internal forum with one's confessor, of receiving the sacraments, provided that no scandal

---

7   The quotation within this quotation is from a homily preached by John Paul II at a synod of bishops in 1980.

was given." His reply was very clear, just like what Pope Francis affirms: There is no general norm that can cover all the particular cases. The general norm is very clear; and it is equally clear that it cannot cover all the cases exhaustively.

This recollection notwithstanding, Cardinal Ratzinger wrote in the 1994 CDF letter clarifying Pope John Paul's words:

> It is certainly true that a judgment about one's own dispositions for the reception of Holy Communion must be made by a properly formed moral conscience. But it is equally true that the consent that is the foundation of marriage is not simply a private decision since it creates a specifically ecclesial and social situation for the spouses, both individually and as a couple. Thus the judgment of conscience of one's own marital situation does not regard only the immediate relationship between man and God, as if one could prescind from the Church's mediation, that also includes canonical laws binding in conscience. Not to recognise this essential aspect would mean in fact to deny that marriage is a reality of the Church, that is to say, a sacrament.

HOLD TO THE PAST IN FAITH

It's no wonder, then, that general discussion today of communion for the remarried has reverted to a reliance on individual conscience without reference to objective norms, when previous rejections of this path, rejections rooted in ontological and Scriptural realities, are never reiterated, never referenced, or are actually misrepresented.

Yet as G. K. Chesterton puts it, the beauty of the Church is that she doesn't discard the past:

> A thing as old as the Catholic Church has an accumulated armoury and treasury to choose from; it can pick and choose among the centuries and brings one age to the rescue of another. It can call in the old world to redress the balance of the new. (*The Catholic Church and Conversion*, 1926)

Cardinal Ratzinger writes of "a matter of a tolerant and benevolent pastoral solution" (that the couple may live as brother and sister) being *consistent* with previous teaching; does *Amoris Laetitia* do the same, or does it stray into *contradicting* previous teaching, reversing the implication of the words "obligation to separate"? Is the document capable of being interpreted as doing so? *Has* it been interpreted as doing so? The answer to the latter question is, simply and demonstrably, yes. The answers to the others become clearer the more we study what the Church has always held.

This question of interpretation and teaching is not an academic one. The "irregularity" spoken of almost half a century ago in *Familiaris Consortio*, whatever the intentions of Pope John Paul II were, has become the "new normal" of today. Given that in 1981 the problem of the divorced and remarried seeking Communion—that is, seeking (or indeed simply assuming) full reception into the life of the parish—was widespread enough to grip the attention of *that* Synod, it seems that now we are dealing with an attempt simply to codify a *de facto* change in doctrine (and by extension, the direct teaching of Jesus Christ Himself).

Professor Jessica Murdoch, in her excellent *First Things* essay, *Creeping Infallibility*, which deals with the question of how to assess the magisterial weight of papal pronouncements, writes:

> One could sum this up by noting that a true development of doctrine—a development that requires full assent of mind and will from the faithful—gives life and vitality to the soul. By contrast, doctrinal evolution in which a new teaching sublates and eliminates the earlier teaching in a quasi-Hegelian

fashion breeds dissolution, confusion, and death.

The death Professor Murdoch speaks of here is the death of the soul, for the teachings of the Church, her permissions, her discipline, and indeed everything she does for the faithful all have the same goal: The salvation of souls by means of keeping intact the vessel of that salvation, the Body of Christ; that is, herself.

The Christian, as I said at the beginning of this discussion, has the duty to remain faithful to the Gospel and to the Creed. John Henry Newman, in his sermon entitled "The Gospel, a Trust Committed to Us," says of Christ's Word:

> If we Ministers of Christ guard it not, it is our sin but it is your loss, my brethren; and as any private person would feel that his duty and his safety lay in giving alarm of a fire or of a robbery in the city where he dwelt, though there were ever so many special officers appointed for the purpose, so, doubtless, every one of us is bound in his place to contend for the Faith, and to have an eye to its safe custody.

He goes on to say:

This Faith is what even the humblest member of the Church may and must contend for; and in proportion to his education, will the circle of his knowledge enlarge. The Creed delivered to him in Baptism will then unfold, first, into the Nicene Creed (as it is called), then into the Athanasian; and, according as his power of grasping the sense of its articles increases, so will it become his duty to contend for them in their fuller and more accurate form. All these unfoldings of the Gospel Doctrine will become to him precious as the original articles, because they are in fact nothing more or less than the one true explanation of them delivered down to us from the first ages, together with the original baptismal or Apostles' Creed itself.

No matter how humble the position of that Christian might be, when he studies God's Word and the Church's teachings, he is correct in reminding our shepherds to guard the flock—and praying that they do. This duty is my reason for contrasting in an explicit way the perennial teaching we have been given on the question of divorce, remarriage, and children with that of *Amoris Laetitia*.

In the Church, authority—even the authority of the pope—depends on its harmony with Sacred Scripture, Tradition, and the Magisterium—the teachings that went before. This is the stable triangle of support that we *must* find amongst the words given to us, or we are right to question them where they touch on the salvation of souls, the Covenant given to us, and our fidelity to God.

APPENDIX 2
Outline of *Casti Connubii*

I. INTRODUCTION

A. The great dignity of marriage, and Christ's intention for it (1)

B. The demands made on man by the dignity of marriage: knowledge of Christian doctrine concerning it, and conformity with that knowledge (2)

C. Occasion for writing: errors (3)

D. Subject of encyclical: nature, benefits, and errors concerning marriage (4)

II. THE ORIGIN OF MARRIAGE (5-9)

A. Origin of marriage

1. God is the primary author of marriage and its laws (5)

2. The human will by its consent is a secondary source (6)

B. Consequence of this for the nature of marriage

2. Conjugal fidelity (19–30)

    a. Conjugal fidelity is justice both towards one spouse and towards God (19)

    b. Elements of conjugal fidelity

        i. Unity (one man and one woman) (20–21)

        ii. Chastity (purity in the relationship between husband and wife) (22)

        iii. Love (23–25)

        iv. Obedience (26–29)

    c. Summary (30)

3. Sacrament (31–42)

    a. Introduction (Sacrament includes indissolubility, and being an efficacious sign of grace) (31)

    b. Indissolubility

        i. Proof of the indissolubility of marriage

           (1). From Christ's words (32)

           (2). From Church's tradition, as expressed in St. Augustine (33)

        ii. Extent of the applicability of indissolubility

           (1). Every marriage is by divine decree

indissoluble at least in
some way (34)

(2). Possibilities for divorce
are based on God's law,
not on human decision
(35)

(3). A consummated
Christian marriage is
absolutely indissoluble

  (a). Consummation
makes a Christian
marriage completely
indissoluble (35)

  (b). Because it signifies
most perfectly
Christ's marriage
with the Church,
which can never be
dissolved. (36)

  iii. Benefits of indissolubility

c. Efficacious sign of grace (one of
the seven sacraments)

  i. Marriage is a sacrament in
strict sense (37)

  ii. Every true marriage
between baptized persons is
a sacrament (38)

  iii. The grace of the sacrament
(39)

    (1). Marital grace is given to

SOURCES

The following sources mentioned in this book are readily available online.

Catechism of the Catholic Church. Promulgated by John Paul II, September 8, 1997.

Congregation for the Doctrine of the Faith. *Letter to the Bishops of the Catholic Church Concerning the Reception of Holy Communion by the Divorced and Remarried Members of the Faithful*, September 14, 1994.

Francis. Apostolic Exhortation *Amoris Laetitia*, On Love in the Family, March 19, 2016.

John Paul II. Apostolic Exhortation *Familiaris Consortio*, On the Christian Family in the Modern World, November 22, 1981. –. Apostolic Letter *Mulieris Dignitatem*, On the Dignity and Vocation of Woman, August 15, 1988.

Murdock, Jessica. "Creeping Infallibility." *First Things*, September 2016.

Paul VI. Encyclical Letter *Humanae Vitae*, On the Regulation of Birth, July 25, 1968.

ABOUT THE AUTHOR

Leila Marie Lawler is married to noted journalist Philip F. Lawler. They live in Central Massachusetts. They have seven children and a goodly number of grandchildren. Leila's website is *Like Mother, Like Daughter* (http://likemotherlikedaughter.org). She is co-author of *The Little Oratory: A Beginner's Guide to Praying in the Home* (Manchester, NH: Sophia Institute Press, 2014) and *The Summa Domestica* — a forthcoming three-volume work presenting the themes explored for more than a decade on her popular blog, which is dedicated to helping parents establish a home, educate their children, and maintain the collective memory.

Printed in the USA
CPSIA information can be obtained
at www.ICGtesting.com
LVHW041057030923
757095LV00006B/219